CURRICULUM BUILDING

in general education

GENERAL EDUCATION SERIES

Institute of Higher Education, EARL J. MCGRATH, *General Editor, Teachers College, Columbia University*

CARPENTER: *The Larger Learning*

CARLIN: *Curriculum Building in General Education*

FISHER: *Humanities in General Education*

HAUN: *Science in General Education*

MAYHEW: *Social Science in General Education*

MORSE-DRESSEL: *General Education for Personal Maturity*

SHOEMAKER-FORSDALE: *Communication in General Education*

CURRICULUM BUILDING
in general education

Edward A. Carlin
Douglas Dunham
Thomas H. Greer
John N. Moore
T. Benson Strandness

EDWARD A. CARLIN and EDWARD B. BLACKMAN
Editors

Wm. C. Brown Company Publishers, *Dubuque, Iowa*

Copyright, 1960
by
Edward A. Carlin

Library of Congress Catalog Card Number: 60-11880

Manufactured by WM. C. BROWN CO. INC., Dubuque, Iowa

Printed in U. S. A.

table of contents

foreword

Twelve years ago when programs of general education were multiplying rapidly in the colleges and universities of this country, the editor of this series of volumes on the general education in major branches of learning conceived the idea that an interchange of experience among institutions would be advantageous to all. Hence, he asked a group of teachers of general education courses to contribute an article on their own programs to be brought together under one cover with other similar institutional statements in the natural sciences, social sciences, humanities, and communications. The four volumes which resulted were widely used not only among institutions which had already inaugurated a program of general studies, but also among those attempting to design such a program suitable to the needs of their own students.

The Wm. C. Brown Company Publishers of Dubuque, Iowa, the publishers of the original volumes, have long felt that they should be brought up to date. Several have been out of print for a period of years. In the time since the books originally appeared, many new programs have come into existence, some in the colleges and universities represented in the earlier volumes, and some in institutions which have launched a general education program in the past decade.

The other volumes in this series consist of a collection of statements about general education courses in one field, such as social science, in a variety of institutions. In each some attention was given by the several authors to the evolutionary changes which occurred since the publication of the earlier volumes in this series more than a decade ago. This volume describes in much greater detail the changes which took place in a single institution, Michigan State University. This state university early developed a strong general education program for all its undergraduate students regardless of their vocational goals. Moreover, an experimental atmosphere prevailed continuously since the day of the initiation of this comprehensive required program of studies.   Hence evaluation led to continuous modification and readjustment.

In recent years more fundamental alterations have occurred in the general education unit at Michigan State University. This volume describes those changes in considerable detail in each of the various major branches of learning.   It is especially useful to other individuals concerned with similar problems because the reasoning behind the changes in philosophy and practice have been set forth.   The impact of the evaluation procedures and results on course construction is also shown.   The volume contains wider implication than some others which deal solely with a general education program in an independent liberal arts college.   At Michigan State University, however, this program must be adjusted to the curricula of many professional schools such as agriculture, business administration and engineering, as well as to the upper division specialties in the liberal arts departments.

Dean Carlin has prepared a volume which will have wide usefulness.   It complements the other volumes in the series which deal mainly with single courses in many institutions.   Those who wish to get this more comprehensive and diversified view of these attempts to provide a suitable general education for American youth will find it in the other six volumes published by the Wm. C. Brown Company Publishers of Dubuque, Iowa.   They are *Sciences in General Education, Humanities in General Education, Social Sciences in General Education, Communications in General Education, General Education for Personal Maturity* and *The Larger Learning.*

Earl J. McGrath
Executive Officer
Institute of Higher Education

preface

The publication in 1955 of *The Basic College of Michigan State* generated a large number of inquiries about the policies and procedures governing the construction of courses in general education. The purpose of the present book is to answer these questions in terms of the special problems faced by each of the departments in the Basic College.*

The authors and editors are grateful to the following members of the faculty of Michigan State University for their criticisms and suggestions: Russell F. Fink, Paul Dressel, C. A. Lawson, Harry H. Kimber, Leo A. Haak, John N. Winburne, Thomas H. Hamilton. Special thanks are due to Barbara Hanna for her patience and skill in the preparation of the manuscript.

---

*After July 1, 1960 the Basic College will be called the University College.

chapter 1

REORGANIZATION OF THE BASIC COLLEGE

*Edward A. Carlin, Dean**

A major administrative reorganization, together with a curricular revision, was proposed by the Dean of the Basic College, approved by the faculty, and placed into operation during a few months in 1952. The chapters that follow this one will explain in some detail the process of curricular revision that occurred in each of the four areas of study that together form the Basic College program. In this chapter the writer will attempt to trace the development of the changes insofar as they affected and were affected by the overall organization and philosophy of the Basic College. To this end, therefore, the program that existed prior to 1952 will be examined briefly; the emergent organization will be explicated; and an attempt will be made to trace the forces that brought about the change.

The Program Prior to 1952

As established in 1944 the Basic College was composed of seven departments offering courses entitled Biological Science, Physical Science, Social Science, Written and Spoken English, History of Civilization, Literature and Fine Arts, and Effective Living. Students were required to complete the course in Written and Spoken English and at least four other courses, including either Literature and Fine Arts or History of Civilization, Social Science or Effective Living, Biological Science or Physical Science. The student's final

---

*The author is Dean of the Basic College, Michigan State University, East Lansing, Michigan.

grade in each course was determined by his performance on a comprehensive examination over the entire year's work. These examinations were prepared by the Board of Examiners in cooperation with departmental committees.

This system of comprehensive examinations included a provision whereby a student could request permission to take the examination in a particular course after he had completed one or two terms or even before he had taken any formal work in the course at all. If his request was granted by the department head and approved by the dean and if he achieved a "C" or better grade on the comprehensive examination, the student received credit for that course.

There were several characteristics of the general education program of the Basic College prior to 1952 that should be mentioned for the purpose of establishing benchmarks for ascertaining the nature and extent of the curricular and organizational change that occurred in 1952. The Basic College was established in 1944 as an autonomous administrative unit of the University, headed by a dean, having its own budget and the power to make faculty appointments within the organization, subject of course to the usual approval by the Board of Trustees. The Basic College was charged with providing a general education for all students regardless of their areas of specialization. It was empowered to and did develop the seven comprehensive courses that have been mentioned above. The course requirements for students were such as to assure that all students would have some experience in communications, the humanities, the natural sciences, and the social sciences. However, within these broad areas students did have a choice. A student might, for example, choose to satisfy the natural science requirement by taking the course in Biological Science or the one in Physical Science. Another important characteristic of the Basic College as initially established was a provision for those students who at the time they matriculated at Michigan State had not yet decided which course of study they wished to pursue for the bachelor's degree. These students were designated "No-Preference" students and were urged to consult with their counselors and to sample various introductory courses during their freshman and part of their sophomore years before indicating their areas of concentration. A further characteristic of the general education program of the Basic College was the assumption that while students would take their general education requirements during the first two years of their college careers they would at the same time begin to take work in the area of eventual concentration.

A more detailed statement concerning the formation of the Basic College in 1944 can be found in the book, *The Basic College of Michigan State*, edited by Thomas H. Hamilton and Edward Blackman. In the chapters that follow this one there will be found more detailed information concerning the nature of the courses themselves, both before and after the 1952 reorganization. The foregoing thumbnail sketch, however, is for the present purpose a sufficient indication of the nature of the program prior to 1952.

The Program Since 1952

Following a transition period during 1952-1953, the curriculum of the Basic College has emerged as four comprehensive courses: Natural Science, Humanities, Social Science, and Communication Skills. All students are expected to complete all four of these courses. Typically, a freshman student will take the course in Communication Skills and the course in Natural Science while the sophomore will enroll in Social Science and Humanities. Certain curricula require that Social Science be taken in the freshman year while others may require that Humanities be delayed until the junior year. Each of these four courses is offered by a separate department. These four departments, together with the Office of Evaluation Services (formerly the Board of Examiners) and the Dean's Office, constitute the organizational structure of the Basic College. The Office of Evaluation Services provides consultant and expert advice to the four departments of the Basic College for the construction and evaluation of term-end examinations. The student's grade in each course is arrived at by combining the grade given to him by his instructor at the end of the term with the grade that he achieves on the final examination. The Office of Evaluation Services, in addition to its examining functions, provides assistance to the departments in the area of educational research.

In the Dean's Office, in addition to a Dean, there is an Assistant Dean in Charge of Student Affairs, who is responsible for all academic actions for freshman and sophomore students; an Assistant to the Dean in charge of research and development, who is responsible for facilitating faculty research of all kinds and for providing advice and consultation for curricular development; and a Coordinator for Continuing Education, responsible for maintaining liaison between the adult education program of the University and the Basic College.

The Process of Curricular Change

If, as was the case, one type of curricular organization existed in the Basic College prior to 1952 and a different one after that date, there is inevitable curiosity concerning the forces — both from within the Basic College and from the University at large — that brought about the change. The primary purpose of this chapter is to discuss the factors that led to the change and the events that marked it.

To attempt to identify a large-scale curricular change with a particular date or event is probably about as accurate as to attribute the cause of the first World War to the assassination of an Austrian archduke. On the other hand, the usefulness of selecting some significant act as a base point for the discussion of change is well recognized. In my judgment, a letter written by the Dean of the Basic College to the President of the University on January 31, 1952, constitutes a point of departure for the discussion and explanation of the large curricular changes that took place in the Basic College during the years 1952 and 1953.

In this letter the Dean recommended a reorganization that would result in the formation of four departments, offering courses entitled Basic Communication, Natural Science, Social Science and Effective Citizenship, and the History of Mankind. He recommended that Basic Communication be a nine-hour course and that the other three courses carry twelve term credits each. In his letter the Dean listed seven reasons for the proposed reorganization. Some of these reasons supported early action on his recommendations because of plans underway in some departments for internal course reorganization and the publication of new materials, the amount of time necessary to get the new program organized and underway, the status of personnel under the tenure rules, and other matters. The most cogent argument for the reorganization in principle, however, was the statement that "our present structure is not defensible. We should have certain areas which are required of all students, which are clearly defined, which are definitely a part of the equipment of *all* college graduates and which can be defended."

One has no great difficulty in identifying the educational philosophy upon which the proposed reorganization rested. The program in existence in the Basic College in 1952 was a modified area elective system. The proposed reorganization would result in an entirely prescribed general education program for all students.

The arguments for and against a completely prescribed general education program are familiar to most educators. Two of them were particularly relevant to the proposed reorganization within the Basic College. One was the large imbalance between the Physical and Biological Science course enrollments. The small enrollments in Physical Science indicated that a large percentage of Basic College students were not being exposed to that important body of knowledge. Another important consideration was that, since students had some choice in courses for the satisfaction of the general education requirement, it was almost impossible for the more advanced and specialized courses to be built on the general education program. The fact that the proposal was made in 1952 rather than at some later date can probably be attributed to several administrative considerations. A department head who had been serving in a dual capacity had asked to be relieved of his responsibilities as head of the Department of Physical Science. In another department a revision of course materials was underway which, if consummated, would in all probability have frozen that department's course for a period of two years. The fact that the entire program was still a comparatively new one suggested that a radical change was possible and was certainly the basis for the judgment that delay would make the process more rather than less difficult.

From a review of the sketchy and incomplete documents in the form of letters, notes, and memoranda that relate to this proposed reorganization and the period extending to its approval by the faculty, it is apparent that matters of both educational philosophy and administrative convenience were involved and that the two were frequently confused. An attempt has been made to separate the two threads, and from that effort the following conclusions seem to be warranted.

It goes almost without saying that the Basic College program established in 1944 was never viewed as immutable. As a matter of fact, reorganization of materials and revision of course outlines had taken place within each of the departments from the very beginning. It is also true that from time to time the question was raised concerning the advisability of offering a general education program that would be the same for all students. Numerous attempts were also made, both through faculty committees and through joint meetings of departmental staffs, to increase the coordination between the various offerings of the Basic College departments. Nevertheless, the proposed merger of seven courses into four came as a surprise and shock to most members of the Basic College faculty. In the ensuing debates over the reorganization three issues can be distinguished.

First, there was the question of whether or not such a reorganization was desirable; second, the question of whether or not it was possible; and third, the question whether the proposal had been properly presented. The first two of these considerations tended to reinforce each other. For example, those members of the Biological Science department who were convinced that the biological sciences and the physical sciences could not be merged into a single program were inevitably convinced that the proposed reorganization was undesirable. Many other faculty members were skeptical about the desirability of the proposed reorganization — that is, they were not opposed to reorganization in principle but they doubted the wisdom of this specific proposal. However, objections were raised more frequently to the way in which the proposal was made than to the nature of the proposal itself. Notwithstanding the facts that the proposal was favorably accepted by the department heads, was accorded a close but nonetheless favorable vote by the Basic College faculty, and was finally accepted by a majority vote of the University faculty, it carried the stigma of administrative fiat and is probably still viewed in this light by some of the faculty even to the present day. Some of the reasons for this are clear. Many are not. In 1952, for example, enrollments were falling and many faculty in the Basic College did not have tenure status. Therefore, when a proposal to merge departments was introduced into this situation, an administrative intent that contributed nothing to faculty security was inferred by many faculty members. The fact that the program was new and was viewed as experimental made for a sensitivity that might not otherwise have been present. Another factor, and perhaps one of the most important in the situation, involved the old, old question of the amount and kind of educational leadership that an administrator may appropriately exert.

chapter 2

COMMUNICATION SKILLS: 1944-1958*

*T. Benson Strandness***

When the Basic College was established in 1944, the freshman language course, then called Written and Spoken English, was the only general education course required of all students. Apparently it was deemed indispensable. Yet there are colleges and universities in which no such course exists — composition, communication, rhetoric, or what you will. At such places, of course, a fair competence in the use of English by entering students must be assumed. It must also be assumed that further development of this competence will be a recognized function of work in all parts of the curriculum. The vast majority of institutions do not feel free to make either of these assumptions. Further-

---

*In 1958-59 a radical revision of the M.S.U. Communication Skills course was undertaken, the nature of which is set forth elsewhere in this series. (See Francis Shoemaker and Louis Forsdale, *Communication in General Education*, chapter on "Communication Skills at Michigan State University" by Frederic Reeve. Dubuque, Iowa: Wm. C. Brown Company Publishers, 1960.) Briefly, as stated for the student in the introduction to his syllabus, it is as follows: "The primary purpose of the course is to help you improve your reading and writing. [Formal instruction in speaking and listening, in other words, has been discontinued.] Its secondary purpose is to give you an opportunity to broaden and deepen your awareness and knowledge of our American heritage. You will improve your ability to read by studying selected documents dealing with living issues of the American past and present. You will improve your ability to write by thinking and talking about these documents and expressing your ideas and reactions to them in a variety of ways." This means that the present essay memorializes a fifteen-year effort at Michigan State to integrate instruction in the four skills of reading, writing, speaking, and listening. It is of more than historical interest, however, for many of the problems it deals with are of perennial concern in any general education course whose aim is to instruct students in the better use and understanding of English; for the course which attempts to combine instruction in the four skills, they are urgent.

**The Author is Professor of Communication Skills, Michigan State University, East Lansing, Michigan.

more, as class size creeps upward under growing population pressure, and as the use of machine-scored examinations becomes increasingly prevalent, the assumptions become less generally tenable each year.

Another reason for requiring special work in language, at whatever level, is that we cannot help feeling that such work is important for the student's mental development. We note the words of Woodrow Wilson: "As a young boy . . . I was taught to think about what I was going to say, and then I was required to say it correctly. Before I was grown, it became a habit."[1] Such habit formation must be our aim, even though accomplishing it is extremely difficult and comparatively rare. On every hand we hear complaints that neither undergraduates nor graduates of our colleges and universities are able to use their mother tongue well, and despite all our efforts, the criticism continues.

In a much-quoted INS feature, for example, Dean William C. Warren of Columbia University's Law School is reported as saying: "We are entitled to expect that the college graduate be able to read argumentative or expository prose swiftly, comprehendingly, and retentively; that he be able to express himself in speech and writing grammatically, literately, and precisely; that he has learned the basic lesson of using a dictionary. But we have found that few of our entering students, however carefully selected, possess these skills to the extent needed for law study." Despite the fact that about eighty per cent of these students had had special training in English composition, Dean Warren expresses dismay with their general inability to write: "Even the most tolerant of critics will concede that whatever be the arts of which the students are bachelors, writing is not one of them. We can't teach them to put their thoughts in order, we cannot teach them grammar; we cannot rectify their clumsy use of language. It is obvious that if we are to require the study of certain subjects as a prerequisite to Law School admission, this must be done with a major emphasis upon writing."[2] If things are bad at the graduate level, they naturally leave something to be desired at the undergraduate as well. Bernard Iddings Bell asserts that among students in one of our

---

[1]David Lawrence, *The True Story of Woodrow Wilson*, George H. Doran, New York, 1924, page 18.

[2]Lansing *State Journal*, Monday, February 6, 1956, page 13.

better state universities "four out of ten could not read quickly or accurately — to say nothing of being able to write correctly — a single paragraph of coherent prose."

In fairness to the nation's teachers of English one must add that when, during the last war, the New York *Times* sponsored an American history quiz for seven thousand freshmen in colleges across the country, student shortcomings in this academic area were also rather startling. (In which would they be otherwise?) Three out of four, for example, did not know who was President during the Civil War. Such ignorance, however, will not cause them nearly so much embarrassment as the belief that Lincoln "emaciated" the slaves. For the latter is a language matter and as such will give them no end of trouble.

We should also remember that linguistic shortcomings in the young are not a source of concern for our society alone. In 1943 a curriculum report appeared in England which noted that "too many pupils show marked inability to present ideas clearly to themselves, to arrange them, and to express them clearly on paper or in speech; they read without a sure grasp of what they read, and they are too often at a loss in communicating what they wish to communicate in clear and simple sentences and in an expressive and audible tone." At about this same time Vladimir Potemkin, People's Commissar of Education, expressed a similar unhappiness over the language habits of Russian youth. Criticism of the same kind is being heard in France and Holland.[3]

But hope springs eternal in the breast of the language arts curriculum builder, and the so-called "communications movement" is a recent manifestation of this fact. Under it has taken place integration of subject matter in such diverse fields as logic, linguistics, psychology, semantics, rhetoric, and communication theory; and work has been combined for teaching the skills of reading, writing, speaking, and listening. Under it, with the founding of the program in general education in the Basic College in 1944, the communication course at Michigan State University was instituted with the title of Written and Spoken English, later changed to Communication Skills.

---

[3]See H. D. Gideonse, "The Coming Showdown in the Schools," *The Saturday Review of Literature*, XXVIII, February 3, 1945, page 6.

Course Development

If, as is sometimes said, the life span of a new idea in an American college is roughly ten years, the course in Communication Skills had by 1958 entered on old age, for unlike the other courses in the Basic College it did not go through a period of reorganization and reappraisal in 1952 and 1953. Perhaps it should have. At any rate, for well over ten years it continued in substantially the same form.

Briefly, that form was as follows: Students normally enrolled in the course for three terms of ten weeks each, five hours a week for three credits a term. The original planning committee for the course stipulated that there be no more than twenty students per section, but the usual pressures gradually raised that level to around twenty-five. The five weekly hours were divided into two single-hour periods of recitation, one two-hour period of writing or reading, and one hour of lecture-listening. In the last named hour an instructor met with his three sections in a suitable auditorium. The hours of recitation were devoted to class discussion, speeches, speech criticism, and testing. Theoretically, the two-hour writing periods were devoted to the study of problems in writing and to the actual writing of papers under the supervision of the instructor. Theoretically also, two-hour reading periods alternated week by week with the writing periods and were devoted to laboratory work in reading. Actually, the pressure of time which resulted from having twenty-five or more students per section caused both of these aims to be compromised in practice.

The first term's work was divided into units dealing with observation, definition, development of ideas, and demonstration. The four facets of communication — reading, writing, speaking, and listening — figured in each unit, the ideal pattern being one in which the student listened and read concerning a subject, then spoke about it, and finally expressed himself in writing.

The work of the second term concerned the nature, creation, and evaluation of reports. Students studied fact, inference, and judgment in reporting, learned to use the library while preparing one or more investigative papers, and became acquainted with newspapers and magazines as instruments of reporting.

The third term's work centered on problem solving (mainly through panel discussions) and persuasion as types of communication.*

Obviously the nature of such a course is barely indicated by a brief description of this kind. If it is really to be understood, at least three things must be considered: course philosophy, teaching staff, and student body.

In curricular development the department tried hard to be democratic rather than authoritarian. Bi-weekly staff meetings (alternating with bi-weekly in-service meetings), a score or more of functioning commitees, course and teacher evaluations elicited from students — all testify to the elaborate and some might say appalling effort to make the enterprise one of staff and student rather than administrative determination. Decisons occasionally came by administrative fiat, but only occasionally and then with a sense of embarrassment.

Somewhat surprisingly perhaps, the amount of staff participation tended to be more a matter for groans than congratulations, and each year brought its crop of requests that the number of staff meetings and committees be reduced. Whatever its price, however, continuing staff participation did produce a psychological unity of immense value; for while individuals were not always happy with decisions reached, they knew they had had their chance to vote and speak their minds.

Such participation was mandatory if course unity was to be established, differences in staff backgrounds reconciled, and training supplied in areas where that of some staff members was strong and that of others weak or non-existent. Unity in diversity was the aim, and it was realized to a surprising degree.

As evidence of the democratic nature of course planning, one chairman of the committee charged with syllabus revision wrote in his annual report to the head of the department: "The committee undertook to keep the staff informed of its progress and to receive approval of its plans. Three progress reports were prepared, presented to the staff, and discussed and voted upon by them. The

---

*For further details regarding course arrangements — texts, statements of objectives, descriptions of the various units of work — the reader should see Chapter 2 of *The Basic College of Michigan State*, Michigan State College Press, East Lansing, 1955.

result is that the decisions embodied in the new syllabus represent ones in which the staff generally concurs." The pattern may be taken as typical for such undertakings in the department.

The Course Philosophy

The professed aims of courses like Communication Skills are generally utilitarian, and rightly so in some degree. But having said this, one must ask what is meant by "utilitarian." As Harold Taylor has remarked, "The study of French can imply its use for calling taxis or for enjoyment of one of the world's great literatures." A teacher cannot say with certainty what the ends of language teaching are, for they are determined by circumstances over which he has little or no control. One occasionally hears of courses in "Industrial Communications," as if this were an isolable field of study. It is not, any more than is "Engineering English," a course once hopefully projected at many institutions but now generally dropped in recognition of the fact that engineers are members of the human race and that verbal abilities know no vocational boundaries.

Unlike something called "Engineering English" or "Industrial Communication," the M.S.U. course in Communication Skills must serve as part of a program of general education. Those who teach it must ask themselves, therefore, what the aims of general education are. The answer usually given is that general education should prepare students for the responsibilities and privileges of life in a free society. Does Communication Skills do this? Not if its concerns are merely with utility.[4]

The General Electric Corporation has distributed a pamphlet to the nation's high schools entitled "Why Study English?" Its authors make the point that what the students accomplish in the study of language will "make all the difference whether they and we or some other company of their choice will succeed together." Such a statement represents the growing conviction on the part of American businessmen and many others as well that the key to both individual and corporate success is the ability to do "the right things" with language.

---

[4]The discussion in this section generally derives from T. B. Strandness, "Skills and Values in the Communication Course," *Journal of General Education*, XI, April, 1956, pages 175-178.

Many teachers of the language arts regard such an endorsement of their efforts with mixed feelings of gratification and distrust. Why distrust? Because they feel that justifying language study in terms of business success alone makes it simply a tool of one's trade, of no more ethical concern than a pencil sharpener, and that to introduce such an approach into the college classroom would be a disgrace. Certainly it would be at odds with a program of general education appropriate to a free society.

Some language arts teachers will settle for the concept of utility. More will not. Granting that the student must find a means of livelihood, the latter group insist that whether or not he can find himself is considerably more important. Such a search demands, they say, the development of his ability to express himself in language. Since man is uniquely a talking animal, self-discovery means discovery in terms of words. An ordered, vigorous, unimpeded relationship of the individual to his world expressed through words: this, they feel, is the communication teacher's concern.

They also insist that the value for the individual of putting things into words has a direct corollary in the value for society in such expression, that the full and unimpeded expression of facts and ideas spells well-being not only for the individual but also for the community which fosters such expression. The good society, they feel, is one in which the channels of communication are kept open as a matter of conscious public policy, one in which secrecy is recognized as a good and early friend of tyranny.

In a less favorable sense, they point out, the closed or servile society is communicative too; it is quite conceivable that just as much speaking, reading, writing, and listening (considerably more listening!) will occur in a highly developed authoritarian society as in a democracy. In certain respects, the language skills required of the qualified servant of autocracy are as definite and demanding as those needed by his democratic counterpart. The mere development of language skill, therefore, is not enough in a general education program devoted to the training of free men. What is needed, they feel, is training which will encourage language habits appropriate to such men.

Such training, as developed in Communication Skills at Michigan State University, concentrated on the student's experience of the natural world, both as he knows it and as he finds it reported to him by others. This is not easy. The student, buffeted by the persuasive forces of a society eager to cut and shape him to size, is generally on his way to becoming merely the well tailored consumer — of soup, automobiles, and ideologies. A sense of discovery of the world around him, the idea that his environment needs continually to be examined and reassessed according to his own standards (not his father's or teacher's), the thought of eagerly exploring the observations and assessments of others as they appear set down in the written word — such things have largely been lost to him. The pressures of a thousand conformities have damaged his impulse to take the measure of things and have put in its place the desire to measure up. The great job of higher education, certainly of general education, is to halt and reverse this transition.

Emphasizing the data of human experience means many things, all of which should find embodiment in Communication Skills. It means assignments which encourage an "itch for reality," a desire to search for what lies behind the abstractions, comfortable generalizations, a priori assumptions, and convenient stereotypes with which every society covers and frequently opposes the workings of change. It argues the benefits of free and candid utterance as opposed to the security of silence and passivity in man's relation to a restless and shifting world. It points the need for demonstration, as opposed to mere assertion, and for the struggle of ideas in the market place. It points the need, too, for such a market place. It suggests that the growing society, like the growing person in that society, is forever in search of knowledge and the means of applying it to the improvement of human institutions. It suggests also that his search is of a kind which can be less well served by polemics than by discussion. It means extending the scientist's caution and hankering for specificity into the verbalized patterns of everyday experience.

An emphasis on the open as opposed to the closed or servile society in the Communication Skills course means facing the fact that men's interpretation of experience will differ and that the uses they make of it will vary between the age-old extremes of generosity and greed, love and hate, cooperation and strife. The free development of the uses of language — that is, freedom of speech, freedom of the press, or any other aspect of freedom in human communication to which the open society subscribes — involves risk, and the language course which pretends to be concerned with more than the mechanics of expression must recognize this risk and assess its results. The assessment is a moral one, for it means examining the uses of language in terms of the human ends of truth, freedom, money, or the power it is made to serve. To be concerned with the debasing of verbal coinage on the advertising page (money) or in the demagogue's utterance (power) is to be ethically concerned. The corruption of language in the hands of those employing it for venal ends means a debasing of the very stuff of human thought. Liberal language study, in short, cannot be undertaken apart from concepts of social responsibility.

Ethics and morality mean little except as they are translated into human behavior, a permeating aspect of which is language. Meaning and method (which is to say behavior) cannot be discussed apart from each other, even though we habitually speak of "skill courses" and "content courses" as if they were separate and distinct. Since Mark Hopkins on one end of a log and a student on the other has so long symbolized the ideal educational enterprise, we should note Bliss Perry's remark that "Dr. Hopkins taught us nothing about the history of philosophy." What he did teach, says Perry, was "how to philosophize." His great success as a teacher lay in his ability to get young men to think. It was the same kind of success which the communication skills teacher feels when a student remarks: "When I came into this course I was mentally comfortable; I do not think I will be quite so comfortable again." For such a student the course has done what college training in any of the liberal arts must aim to do: It has got him to take a fresh look at the world around him.

In short, being part of a general education program means for the communication course that it must show itself to be a liberal, which is to say, a liberating enterprise. The matter of utility versus disinterestedness, of skills versus values, would seem to carry a double lesson. Those who want language study to be merely practical in its ends must look to what they mean by practicality. On the other hand, advocates of disinterestedness damage their efforts if they deprive such study of a working function in their students' lives.

The Student

If what he has just read seems to the reader somewhat top-lofty or excessively idealistic, let him be reassured, for both of these things are prevented in the workaday classroom by the presence of many students who have had an absolute minimum of formal language training. Some have not written more than three or four papers during their entire high school career; many have never read a serious book outside of the classroom, have never seen a play, never used a library, never spoken in public.

The effect on the work of the course is often painful, much more so than the effect of a comparable inadequacy on a course in history, say, or one in political science. For time given to speaking assignments depends largely on the students for its success. The student whose capacities or preparation is weak inflicts a far greater burden on the class than he does where oral participation is largely voluntary and where, as a result, the best students participate a good deal and the weakest not at all.

Plainly the difficulties which the language arts course faces are great and to some extent unique. Two things would seem to be essential: (1) recruitment of teachers and funds to the end that class size may be held down to approximately twenty students[5] and (2) sectioning of students to suit varying needs and abilities, a subject to which we will later return.

The Instructor

A few years ago the chairman of the Conference on College Composition and Communication reminded that organization[6] that both logic and common sense would seem to indicate the wisdom of strengthening the field in which "sixty per cent of the college teaching of English in our country occurs." He was referring to courses in composition and communication.

It would indeed seem reasonable that appropriate graduate programs would pay attention to training people for this work. Generally speaking, however, they do not, because teaching the

---

[5]For the professional consensus on this point, see "Administering the Freshman Course." *College Composition and Communication,* VII, October, 1956. page 127.

[6]Letter of February 12. 1955.

freshman course has generally been regarded as a mere stepping stone to something else. One English instructor expressed the traditional attitude as follows: "Teaching freshman composition thus must remain a not-too-demanding way of earning a living while the beginning instructor gives his primary attention . . . to getting his degree, preparing learned articles, and generally getting ready to teach advanced courses. I am therefore suggesting that, under present conditions, insofar as a graduate student or beginning instructor spends time with a training course and gives more than the minimum required time to teaching freshman composition, he is doing hurt to his professional career. Willfully to do such hurt is manifestly foolish."[7]

There would seem to be, as this writer says, no hope of solving the dilemma "under present conditions." A significant thing about the postwar development of communication skills programs was that in some places, as at Michigan State, they brought about a change in the conditions. This change was primarily the result of abandoning the traditional composition course, putting a more ambitious language course in its place (frequently, as at Michigan State, as part of a program in general education), and offering the teachers of that course the same opportunities for promotion and pay that apply in other fields of academic endeavor.

This improvement in the professional status of the language teacher was accompanied by an awareness of the need for him to be trained realistically for his job. Here again, however, the dilemma presented itself of a felt need on the one hand and, on the other, a traditional inability or disinclination on the part of graduate schools to satisfy it. How shall a Department of Communication Skills secure an adequately trained staff? One can, of course. ignore the problem, give a program the name of "communication," and simply pretend that the teacher is prepared to do his job. But honestly facing the question means choosing between the traditional course taught by persons with traditional backgrounds or a new kind of course taught by a new kind of

---

[7]The article appears in *College Composition and Communication*, October. 1951.

person. A substitute for this second alternative is to use persons with traditional backgrounds in speech, literature, linguistics, philosophy, psychology, anthropology, or what have you, and provide necessary additional training through "in-service" programs. Such, for the most part, was the method at Michigan State.

Some of the announced objectives of the in-servce training program as it was originally established are as follows: "(1) To develop leadership, scholarship, and interest in the Basic Communications Program. (2) To provide an opportunity for staff members to exchange information about the work in which they are engaged. (3) To provide a workshop for the investigation of problems in the general field of communication. (4) To provide an opportunity for presenting the philosophy and aims of the course to both new and old members of the staff. (5) To provide the staff with such knowledge and skills as will enable them to perform more effectively as teachers of Basic Communications."

More specifically, one year's program consisted of the following:

Fall Term

"Objectives of In-Service Training" (Talk by Department Head).

"Communications in Labor Management Relations" (Speaker from outside the department).

"Semantics in Basic Communications" (Speaker from outside the department).

"Evaluation in Basic Communication" (Speaker from outside the department).

"Integration in Basic Communication" (Speaker from outside the department).

"Blockages and the Teaching of Communication" (Speaker from outside the department).

"The Philosophy of General Education" (Talk by the Dean of the Basic College).

"Comprehensive Examinations in the Basic College" (Talk by Head of Board of Examiners).

"Grading Papers for Teaching" (Talk by member of the department).

"Teaching the Unit on Demonstration" (Panel discussion by three members of the department).

Winter Term

"Rudolph Flesch's *The Art of Plain Talk*" (Report by member of the department).

"A Philosophy of Correctness in English Usage" (Speaker from outside the department).

"Shall and Will" (Speaker from outside the department).

"The Subjunctive" (Speaker from outside the department).

"Approaches to Language" (Talk by member of the department).

"Evaluating the Use of Language" (Speaker from outside the department).

"Teaching Vocabulary" (Symposium by members of the department).

"Improving Reading Skills" (Talk by Head of Reading Clinic).

"A Report on a Survey of Communications Courses Conducted by a Joint Committee of the Speech Association of America and the National Council of Teachers of English" (Report by head of the department).

"The Larger Aspects of Communication" (Talk by member of the department).

Spring Term

"A Philosophy of Self-Expression" (Talk by Department Head).

"More Suggestions for Helping Students Improve Their Reading" (Talk by Head of Reading Clinic).

"A Report on Howell's *Problems and Styles of Communication*" (Staff symposium).

"Language and Society" (Speaker from outside the department).

"The Colgate Communication Course" (Speaker from outside the department).

"Generalizations on Communication" (Speaker from outside the department).

"The Influence of Language on Student Growth" (Speaker from outside the department).

"A report on Wendell Johnson's *People in Quandaries*" (Staff symposium).

"Improving the In-Service Training Program" (Staff discussion).

When, as was several times the case, course revision of some kind was underway, in-service meetings were frequently devoted to reports from the departmental curriculum committee and to a discussion of ways and means of improving the course. A standard part of in-service training, also, was staff rating of four or five student speeches or themes followed by a tabulation and discussion of results.

In-service programs can be judged only in subjective and speculative terms, but it may fairly be said that over a period of years the weekly staff and in-service meetings accomplished the kind of "unity in diversity" without which a hopeless and fatal fragmentation must have taken place, diversity in staff background being what it was. For most staff members a jealous identification with this or that specialized graduate field gradually disappeared and they became teachers not of this or that one but of all the language arts.

Writing

If a growing unity in staff attitudes and practices is possible, a certain amount of ingrained diversity is both inevitable and desirable. As regards both writing and speaking, but more particularly writing, any group of language teachers finds itself in continuing debate over at least three issues: the kind of writing and speaking which should be expected, the definition of standards of "correctness," and the nature of speaking and writing assignments. The last of these concerns whether assignments should be immediate or derived; that is, whether they should mainly depend on the speaker's or writer's own experience and observation or derive primarily from his reading. The course in which the student's writing and speaking derive from his study of literature depends almost entirely on the latter. A course which is less definitely identified with a particular body of subject matter will tend to emphasize the former, as did the course at Michigan State.

Both types of assignments have good justification. Those who favor assignments based on historical and literary material argue that they give the student "something to think about" and consequently something to say. Those who favor assignments based primarily on the student's own experience point out that such experience is the speaker's and writer's best resource and that for him to learn to use it is one of the most important things he can do in developing intellectual self-reliance. The weakness in this type of assignment, others point out, is that if the student's personal resources are meager he will not be able to achieve very much — or so at least it will seem to those who must read what he writes and listen to what he has to say. Better, they say, to have him parrot Socrates than utter banalities in the name of self-reliance. So the argument continues. The immediate or student-centered type of assignment dominated through most of the years of the Michigan State course, but exponents of the derived or readings-centered type of assignment have persisted and appear recently to have gained the advantage.

The argument concerning "minimum essentials" and prescriptive grammar has dwindled in recent years with the growing impact of modern linguistic study on staff thinking. The teacher who can be characterized merely as a "comma hound" is happily becoming quite rare; each year the student who has something to say and can say it with force and clarity is more likely to score above his mechanically correct but fatuous brother. As one staff member has remarked, "When we come to understand that acceptable usage is a matter of collective agreements, that clarity is more important in language than erudition, and that a moment of sincerity is worth a lifetime of correctness, we will save a lot of wear and tear on our nerves and be better prepared to instruct students in the art of using words effectively in saying what they have to say."[8]

Such an attitude among teachers of the course means that a student learns the difference between correctness and appropriateness. He is instructed concerning varieties in usage and is encouraged to note these varieties in the language of persons around him. He comes to see that he cannot be provided simply with four rules for one thing and three for something else, that instead he must rely on his own and others' actual observation of language use. Above all, he comes to regard language not as a strait jacket — the common attitude and the curse of the English classroom — but as a human, unregimented, frequently erratic thing, the study of which is not an inhibiting but a liberating enterprise. He comes to see that clarity, substance, and vividness in what he has to say

---

[8]C. Merton Babcock, *Basic College Quarterly*, Spring, 1959, page 27.

are the important things, not the forms of the subjunctive or the distinctions between shall and will, that recognizing jargon when it raises its woolly head is more important than spotting gerunds in Webster's "Reply to Hayne," and that the ability to be specific means infinitely more than the avoidance of "ain't."

Although the college student is generally convinced that what he needs is "more grammar," the fact is that he long ago learned just about all the grammar he ever will. What he may possibly now learn is how to express himself with greater effectiveness, personal confidence, and social awareness. His first reaction to such an attitude on the part of the teacher is generally one of some incredulity followed by a feeling of "I did not know English could make so much sense." Sometimes, of course, a student who has difficulty in ordering his thoughts, or, what is more likely, in having significant thoughts to order, remains convinced that what he needs is "more grammar."

But while staff consensus came to oppose the dogmas of prescriptive grammar, it remained uncertain as to what sort of writing and speaking — particularly writing — is appropriate for a general education course in language. The stated aims of such courses generally shun "literary" in favor of the "practical" as the kind of student performance which must necessarily be aimed at. The idea seems to be that students should be fitted with the linguistic equivalent of a stout pair of walking boots as opposed, say, to dancing slippers.

Those who oppose this view argue that while a course with workaday assignments in exposition will not aim to produce short stories, poems, or dramas, it is nonetheless true that wit, vigor, and incisiveness are valued commodities wherever we find them. The fact that "realistically" they are not often found in the writing of students, teachers, or anyone else, does not, they say, make them any less desirable and certainly should not eliminate them as aims to be pursued.

What was the general emphasis in the department? It would be difficult to say, for so long as the instructor operated within the framework of the course syllabus, this was a matter for him alone to decide. Both points of view had their determined advocates, and the work proceeded in an atmosphere of reasonably harmonious diversity.

Reading

The same debate goes on about reading, with the same questions being raised and the same answers given. Here again it is clear that the language course has a double function to perform, one vocational or practical and the other disinterested or humane. Reading is of two kinds: the kind we do because we like to (or can learn to like to) and the kind we do because we must. The number who read because they like to is unfortunately small compared with those who read because they must, as part of their job. This is true among all social groups, college teachers included.[9]

Another fact of practical significance is that many adults with good intelligence and cultural background perceive the printed page poorly. It is not only Johnny who has difficulty with reading but his older brother, his father, his sister, his mother, and his uncle as well. *The New Republic* recently quoted former Senator William Benton as saying that we are "a nation of reading cripples" and noted that more than five thousand officers in the Defense Department have been classified as "slow readers." To improve their skill they have been sent to school one hour a day for thirty days. The result of this intensive effort has been the same as for all such efforts in reading laboratories around the country, including that at Michigan State: a general doubling of reading rate without decline in comprehension.[10]

The teacher with a background in the humanities usually takes a dim view of such statistical accomplishments. He quotes Picasso to the effect that when you are painting a lovely woman you don't use a tape measure. Reading for him is a matter not of utility but delight. He loves it and has no wish to measure it. Furthermore, reading to him — reading that really counts, that is — means literature, and he takes it very seriously. The utilitarian teacher reminds him, however, that his attitude is one that few of his students can be brought to share and that, moreover, it may be inadequate to their working needs. He is "realistic" and inclined to feel that literature has no place in the language skills

---

[9]See Chapter I of *Adult Reading*, Fifty-Fifth Yearbook of the National Society for the Study of Education, part III, ed. Nelson B. Henry, University of Chicago Press, 1956.

[10]"Reading Cripples," *The New Republic*, CXXXVI, March 4, 1957, page 5.

classroom.   His humane opponent, troubled but at the same time
unwilling to admit this, shifts his position without abandoning
it.   If the absolute or belletristic approach is inappropriate, he
says, the functional one certainly is not.   Under it students read
literature less as literature than as a source of ideas and illustration.
Hiroshima provides an excellent case study in reporting.   So, in a
different way, does Orwell's *1984*.   Allen's *Only Yesterday* is useful in teaching the investigative paper both as a source of topics and
as an illustration of how source materials can be brought to life
by an expert.   Maugham's *Of Human Bondage* is a rich mine of
provocation and illustration; read by all students in a class it can
enrich the work of the term immensely.   Such books as *Knock on
Any Door* (juvenile crime), *The Troubled Air* (censorship), *The
Grapes of Wrath* (migratory labor), *Darkness at Noon* (the meaning of communism), *Native Son* (American race relations), all provide valuable background and stimulation for group discussion.   In
fact, the use of such material is in line with what we know about
the nature of successful discussion.[11]

Was such collateral reading a standard part of the course?
For some teachers, yes.   For others, no.   Here again, where there is
a division in staff attitude, the departmental policy has been to
reach agreement on minimal activities and objectives for the various
units and, beyond that, encourage the instructor to use such methods
as satisfy him best.

One shortcoming of collateral reading is that it does not provide the kind of laboratory training in reading appropriate to the
skills approach.   The problem of introducing such training into
the course is mainly one of time — so much to do with so many
in so few hours a week.   It is also one of equipment.   Tachisto-
scopes, developmental reading manuals, training films, while not
indispensable, are valuable adjuncts to the training effort — adjuncts of a kind which a football coach, say, would probably not
be without.   Lacking them, the language teacher must take such
time as he can afford to develop an awareness of what skillful
reading is.   If he can do this, he has accomplished no small thing,
for the most elaborately equipped reading laboratories have dis-

---

[11]See Irving J. Lee, *Customs and Crises in Communication*, Harper, New
York, 1954, Introduction.

covered that it is the most important factor in developing skill —
more important than all the gadgets.

One should not leave the subject of reading without men-
tioning the advent of the paperbacks. It is no exaggeration to say
that the process of making books available to all who would read
them, begun by Gutenberg, has now been completed by the publishers of the ubiquitous pocket-format books. The kind of corollary reading just discussed would not have been possible ten or
twelve years ago. At that time, in fact, it was specifically dis-
allowed in the Communication Skills course on the ground of cost
to the student.

Such an objection no longer obtains. Unlike Chaucer's scholar,
today's student need not deprive himself that he might have "twenty
bokes, clad in black and red." In the phenomenal rise of the
paperback with its mass distribution methods and low-cost publishing techniques, we have entered the flivver era in book publishing.
As the Model "T" made it possible for just about everyone to own
a car, so the paperback makes it possible for just about everyone to
possess the books he wants to read.

The paperback development clearly promises much that is
both hopeful and good for the language arts curriculum. Just as
clearly, it presents its share of those unattractive characteristics which
follow the popular determination of standards in any of the communication media, be it radio (soap opera), newspapers (the tab-
loid), magazines (stereotyped fiction of the pulps and the slicks),
or whatever. An important part of the teacher's job is to develop
in his students a critical awareness as regards these media, and a
realization that they perform in the role of society's most potent
critics when they do or do not read, look, listen, or buy.

Speaking

A primary question which faces the planner of the freshman
English course is whether or not speaking should be taught in
conjunction with the other language arts. The original framers
of the course at Michigan State answered this question in the
affirmative and the teachers of the course have had little inclination
to question the theoretical rightness of that decision. Whether or
not it is entirely practicable is another matter. As a former head
of the department has noted, "No one has as yet devised a method

of teaching speech except to get students on their feet in the presence of their classmates and instructor for the purpose of making speeches. Speeches must be constructively criticized by the instructor and classmates while the experience is still fresh. Most of this criticism should be done orally so that all students may benefit." He explained that whereas the teaching of writing demands a good deal of time outside of class, speaking consumes "an enormous amount of in-class time. If an assignment calls for a round of three-to-four minute extemporaneous speeches, and there are twenty-five students in the class, the instructor who adheres to the principles of sound speech pedagogy cannot plan on completing the round in much less than four fifty-minute class periods. If the minimum of five speeches per student per quarter is called for in classes that average twenty-five students each, the course must allow for approximately twenty fifty-minute periods."[12]

Can the use of such a number of hours be defended if it means a comparative neglect of, say, reading? As class size has crept upward under increasing population pressures, the urgency of the question has also mounted. Instructors of long experience in the course are generally of the opinion that here is a case where quantitative changes become qualitative as well. The difference, they contend, in attempting an integrated program of language study with a class of twenty-three as opposed to one of twenty-eight is as definite as it is dismaying. Furthermore, they say that it is not a difference which can be eliminated by cutting down on the number of required speeches. A simple but to many unsatisfactory answer to the problem is simply to abandon any effort to give speech instruction in the freshman language course.

Historically, the justification for combining speaking and writing is considerable. When, in 1674, the Harvard Corporation voted "that all undergraduates declaiming in their usual courses in the hall shall, after their said declamations have ended, deliver a copy of each of them fairly written unto the president or senior fellow then present unless they have before showed it their tutor for his perusal,"[13] they were simply voicing the established, indeed

---

12See *The Basic College of Michigan State*, Michigan State College Press, East Lansing, 1955, page 41.

13John Wozniak, "English Composition in Eastern Colleges: 1850-1940," Unpublished Dissertation, Johns Hopkins University, 1951, page 7.

ancient, attitude toward rhetorical instruction. When the famous Boylston Professorship for Rhetoric and Oratory was established at Harvard in 1804, it was for instructing "the students of the several classes in the nature, excellence, and acquisition of the important art of Rhetoric . . . or in the theory and practice of writing and speaking well."[14]

During the latter half of the nineteenth century, the growing emphasis on the art of elocution caused rhetoric to turn more and more toward criticism and composition, a trend which culminated in Barrett Wendell's *English Composition,* published in 1891. From Wendell's famous "English A" derived the type of course which came to be known generally as "Freshman Composition."

So long and flourishing was the reign of this kind of course that challenging it was like challenging the stars in their courses. That it was in fact challenged, however, anyone who is interested may learn by looking through some of the early volumes of the *English Journal,* publication of the National Council of Teachers of English.[15] It is an instructive experience and one that should unsettle those who feel that with the advent of communication courses we entered a markedly new era in teaching the language arts. This is not to suggest that there have been no significant developments in such courses. Interest in general semantics, increased awareness of the role of mass media in our present-day culture, impatience with the prescriptive approach of the older handbooks, recognition of the meaning of group dynamics as concerns man's use of language, sensitivity to propaganda techniques — these are just a few of the things that have brought marked changes in many programs which have been developed. It is to suggest, however, that the jurisdictional contest which has engaged speech and English departments during the last forty years or so has made it convenient to ignore the fact that whatever the new developments in language instruction may be, integration of work in writing and speaking is not one of them.

Theoretically as well as historically the combining of writing and speaking has much justification. The student who speaks to his fellow students addresses a real audience, whereas the student as

---

[14]*Records of Overseers,* IV, Cambridge, 1804, page 402.

[15]See T. B. Strandness, "Perspective and Personnel in Communication Courses," *College Composition and Communication,* VII, February, 1956, 9-10.

writer finds it hard to avoid the feeling that he is engaged in a piece of make believe. Furthermore, the student who speaks before he writes on a subject can receive criticism which will help him in his writing, criticism which, in fact, may be more valuable to him than that which he gets on the writing itself. One is critcism before, the other criticism after the fact.

A common objection to the introduction of speech into the freshman language course is that instead of students giving speeches they will merely present "themes standing on their hind legs." But given a teacher of some competence, there is no reason why this should happen. It is true that the aims of the communication teacher may be somewhat different from those of the regular speech instructor. The staff of Communication Skills early decided that their job was not to train orators or polished platform speakers, although they recognized that this kind of training might frequently be helpful to particular students. The goal, rather, was to develop in students the ability to express themselves in the presence of others with poise and confidence, to organize their thoughts, to speak so that they could be heard and understood, to be aware of their audience, and to know what characterizes responsible speech behavior. The kind of speaking they should be prepared for is the kind they will do as members of a political party, PTA, labor union, or farm organization. Few instructors devoted attention to gestures as such, but neither did they ignore them. Similarly, while they ordinarily avoided exercises aimed at producing "pear-shaped vowels," they did not ignore such matters as articulation and voice quality, especially if they were such as to interfere with effective communication.

Listening

Must we teach listening? One may ask the question with some astonishment — like the Italian lady who said, "In America it is necessary to teach speaking?" A qualified affirmative may be given to both questions. Not that speaking or listening *must* be taught — any more than any other aspect of language must be taught, but those who advocate such training say that these things may be taught with point, that there is justification for study concerning them, that there is awareness to be gained and skills to be learned. The point in this kind of training is illustrated, they say, in a conversation between a Hindu and an American teacher about literacy in their two countries. The Hindu teacher listens to the American's suggestions for the elimination of illiteracy in India and replies, "We should welcome your help. Perhaps we have something to offer in return. For while I regret the inability of many of my people to read and write, yet we must consider further the meaning of literacy. In the United States you measure literacy by the written word. In India we have literacy of the spoken word — thoughtfully spoken and thoughtfully listened to."[16]

Do we possess such literacy, ask the advocates of listening training, when a study of Michigan State University students shows that about three out of four are unable to report the structure of a well organized lecture? Do we possess the literacy of the "unread" Greeks educated through the spoken word? For them an important means of "publication" was the public recital, as by Herodotus of his *History*. Can it be denied that an addiction to the printed page has resulted in a kind of ear-blindness — especially on the part of those who call themselves language teachers? Advocates of listening training suggest that we read a passage of fair difficulty to a class of students and ask for a report on it; the results, they feel sure, will both startle and instruct us. They ask, finally, that we consider what present-day linguistic science has to say about the auditory basis of language learning and, further, to consider what this may logically mean for language teaching.

In answer to such questions, the original framers of the Communication Skills course entered training in listening as one of the course objectives. The attempt to provide such training has fallen into three major phases. In the first, despite misgivings of the designated departmental committee over what it termed "the dearth of scientific knowledge on the subject," plans were made for a course of lectures to be given in the fifth hour of each week on such subjects as would provide background for the study of language and communication. With some slight change from term to term lecture subjects ran as follows (designated instructors giving the lectures several times a week to large numbers of students

16See A. Steiner, K. Sanders, M. Kaplan, "Skill in Listening." National Council of Teachers of English pamphlet, 1944, page 5.

at appointed hours): "Course Orientation," "The Origin of Language," "The Symbolic Nature of Language," "The Science of Language," "Language and Adjustment," "Levels of Usage," "The Dictionary"; in the second term: "Use of the Library," "Radio as Communication," "Public Speaking as Communication," "Newspapers as Communication," "Magazines as Communication," "Sources of Ideas," "Fact and Opinion"; in the third term: "Response to Verbal Symbols," "Propaganda Techniques," "Types of Evidence," "Analysis of a Propaganda Campaign," "Discussion Demonstration," "Public Opinion," "Psychological Barriers to Effective Communication," "Language Barriers to International Understanding."

After several years with such a program the staff agreed that more attention should be given to listening *per se*, at first in conjunction with the established lecture materials and later on a more extensive basis. The program that resulted ran approximately as follows. In the first term: "Introduction to the Course," "Listening as a Means of Learning," "Developing Ideas," "Recognizing Thought Patterns," "Characteristics of the Good Listener," "Listening for Understanding," "Kinds of Listening," "Heilman Listening Test" (two weeks), "Taking Lecture Notes," "Analysis of Listening Habits"; in the second term: "The Nature of Reports," "Projection in Listening" (two weeks), "Oral Reporting" (two weeks), "Aids for Listening Comprehension," "Listening to Radio Reporting" (two weeks), "Listening to Persuasive Reports," "Term-end Listening Test"; in the third term: "Overview of the Term," "Solving Personal Problems," "Solving Group Problems," "Generalizations," "Inductive and Deductive Reasoning," Causal Relations," "Evaluating Persuasion," "Authority and Statistics," "Analogy," "Term-end Listening Test." In each case instruction was brief and application (through the use of news commentaries, lectures, group discussions, etc.) extensive.

The reaction of many staff members to this program was one of indignant protest, expressed in such terms as "repetitious," "dull," and "trivial." It was ultimately abandoned, therefore, as a department-wide undertaking, and instructors were given free reign to handle the "fifth hour" as they saw fit, with the understanding that instruction in listening would be given appropriate attention in the work of the course.

Evaluation

Can listening be taught?   Indeed, one might ask whether any of the language arts can be taught *per se*.   In Wendell Johnson's words, "We don't write writing."   Neither do we speak speaking, listen listening, or read reading, though the attempt is often made to develop ability in these ways.   Language learning is not an isolated thing but a function of intellectual development.   The reading habits of many students, for example, will improve significantly simply because they are in college, not because they have received special instruction in reading.[17]

Instruction in the language arts suffers from what might be termed the great curricular fallacy.   When a situation presents itself which requires remedy, the American's first impulse is to "pass a law" or "require a course."   The faith we put in a course requirement is touching and fantastic.   One extreme result is the idea that without formal instruction in a thing, we can hardly be qualified to speak or act concerning it — the reverse of which is the belief that if a person is qualified in something he must have taken a course in it.   We need to ponder Sir Richard Livingstone's remark that "The good schoolmaster is known by the number of valuable subjects he declines to teach."   It is not inconceivable that some of the subjects to which he refers are in the field of language.   For while the remarkable curricular proliferation which gathers today under the name of "English" is of fairly recent origin, the knowledge of English language and literature is as old as the race.   Let us not deceive ourselves.   Were all English courses erased from our college catalogues the nature of human society would not be drastically altered.   Work in the language arts may be important; it is not indispensable.

Because we cherish an exaggerated concept of what it is, or should be, possible for a course like Communication Skills to do, it persistently disappoints just about everyone concerned.   A Dean of Engineering arrives at a school with a communication type of freshman course from a school (one of the best in the country) with a traditional type of freshman course.   He hopes that the communication course will work the miracle for his engineering

---

[17]See M. E. Gladfelter, *Change in Reading Ability of 474 Students during Freshman Year of College*, Multigraphed Dissertation, University of Pennsylvania, 1945, page 86.

students which the other had. not. It doesn't, and now in his disappointment he looks to the establishment of a special course (just one course, naturally!) for engineers. Maybe *that* will work the needed miracle.

A pre-law student says of his freshman English work, "I don't feel the course did enough for me." Knowing that his efforts in the course had been feeble at best, his teacher reminds him that the first law of learning is that what a man learns he must learn for himself. He had been in the army for three years knowing that he would enter the pre-law curriculum. Had he done anything about improving his ability to use the English language during this time? No, he had not. What he had done was confidently — and, doubtless, somewhat belligerently — wait for the course (the one course!) which would do the job for him. Once again, the hoped for miracle had not occurred. The required English course for him, as for so many, was something you "took" — like a tetanus shot: and while the experience might not be pleasant, it was happily brief. Furthermore, once having taken it, you were protected against lockjaw and writer's cramp for goodness knows how long. One sometimes wishes to say to students what Sinclair Lewis said to a group at the University of Minnesota who had presented themselves in his classroom because they wished to learn to write: "If you want to learn to write," he said, "what the hell are you doing here?"

The extent to which the Lewis line of reasoning may be realistically applied to Freshman English is, of course, a question. In some form or other the course will continue to be offered, students will be required to take it, and teachers will do their best to teach it. And amidst all their discouragements they can feel assured that ultimately the values of their efforts will be recognized. A New York *Times* article by Benjamin Fine[18] reports that "In a survey made by the General Electric Company of more than 13,500 college graduates employed by them, men and women from more than 600 American colleges and universities and nearly equally divided between engineers and non-engineers, the great majority of the non-engineers reported that their most helpful and valuable college subject was 'English communication.' Both writ-

---

[18]December 2, 1956, Section IV, page 11.

ten and spoken English were cited as of extreme value. . . . Engineers on the other hand listed English second to mathematics in importance." The subject most frequently recommended by these college graduates for young high school graduates entering college and aspiring to positions of responsibility in industry was, again, "English communication."

This kind of report comes to English teachers as something of a shock, however pleasant. For while statistically significant and even impressive gains are achievable in the receptive skills of reading and listening, the situation as regards the expressive skills of writing and speaking, is embarrassingly otherwise. Gains in these areas remain a matter of uneasy conjecture. As Norman Foerster has observed, "Even when specific standards for scoring are agreed upon in advance, the consistency or agreement among different readers has been found to be so low as to make the typical theme exercise useless as a dependable index of the student's skill in writing."[19] The same applies to the typical classroom exercise in speech.

But whatever the difficulties of evaluation, it is a work that must be pursued. Students want it and society demands it; it is the teacher's job to do the best he can. At Michigan State as elsewhere this means conferences with students, in-service training devoted to grading, team scoring, composite scoring (that is, scoring arrived at by both subjective and objective methods), and an earnest inquiry into what has been written on the subject of measurement.

So at least say the measurement enthusiasts, who feel that if something has been learned it can be measured — if not right now, then eventually. But teachers of the language arts, like most persons of humane background, tend to be bored and even angered by talk of "error quotients" and "coefficients of correlation." Statistics to them are like a sieve, which can indeed dredge up something from a river but which must always allow what is essentially "river" to escape. Education for them is "what the student has left after he has forgotten what he learned." How, they ask, is one to measure this "what is left"? A student who has read the

[19]See "Teaching the College Student to Write," E. J. McGrath, ed., *Communication in General Education*, Dubuque, William C. Brown Co., 1949, page 51.

Book of Job may be able to recite the trials visited upon that long-suffering man, but will anyone who does not have what Erich Fromm calls "fantasies of omniscience" attempt to measure the result of this reading experience? Who can say what the effect of a particular writing assignment is on a student? True, we give him a grade on his performance, but may not that be largely irrelevant? Suppose we are unable to show that his writing has improved, which is the case more often than not? Should work in writing then be abandoned, or, in the words of the *Harvard Report*, is it nevertheless justified because we wish to provide "at each stage of maturity some continuing contact with liberal and humane studies"?[20] If we are to be guided in our course offerings simply by statistical results, are we to say that "And Sudden Death," the most widely read magazine article ever published, was a failure because it had no perceptible effect on the number of persons killed on our nation's highways? Or, for that matter, is pragmatic America inclined to abandon its work in driver-training for the same statistical reason? How does one justify, statistically, reading Hamlet or writing a poem?

Plainly, the debate here again is between men of fact and men of feeling, advocates of value and those who insist on utility. In reality, however, things are not nearly so simple: the argument is less between men — though that is the form it commonly takes — than it is between the contradictions which inhere in the fact that the communication skills teacher stands with one foot in the liberal arts ("It's a humanities course") and the other in vocational studies ("It's a service course"). This means, as regards the assigning of grades, that he must face both his student and himself with the inadequacy as well as the inevitability of the effort and then do the best he can. As Paul Dressel, former Head of Michigan State's Office of Evaluation Services, recently wrote, "A decision must be made as to whether grades, credits, and the usual academic rigmarole will be perpetuated. They will be. Accepting this, we should assign grades based upon knowledge and upon those intellectual skills for which correctness and accepted standards provide the possibility of reasonably consistent evaluation for all individuals. It should be handled in the most ex-

[20]Page xiii.

peditious and inconspicuous fashion possible, with the teacher emphasizing ungraded outcome and working out means whereby students may evaluate their own progress toward these goals. Such a conception implies a far different attitude toward examinations, toward grading, and toward student-teacher relations than is commonly found in our classrooms."[21]

John Andrew Rice, one of the founders of Black Mountain College, asked John Dewey how a good educational program could be kept from sinking after a few years into the usual institutional coma. "As long as you keep your eye on the individual," said Dewey, "that won't happen." In a course like Communication Skills, where scores of teachers teach thousands of students in literally hundreds of sections, the danger that the individual will be lost sight of is patently very great. Such a course, particularly when it is necessary that everyone follow the same course of study, would seem almost certain to become impersonal and monolithic. In the absence of a conscious and continuing opposing effort, it will do just that.

For many years the student who was poorly qualified for the work of the course was enrolled, voluntarily or involuntarily, in an "Improvement Service." Meanwhile he carried on in the regular work of the course. More recently he has been required to take preliminary, non-credit work in "Preparatory English." In the face of approaching shortages in plant and personnel one must ask whether or not such efforts are justified. Some institutions have decided that they are not, and they have good reasons for their decision, the most cogent being that the poorly qualified student, particularly in writing, has only about one chance in four of emerging into his senior year of college work. Many, however, will not accept this reason as final. It is at least arguable, they say, that in a society which needs trained personnel as much as does ours, it is important if we bring through to graduation only five or ten per cent of those not initially qualified for college work.

If the present great talent hunt offers some justification for clinic services, it offers even more for classes which give special attention to the student of superior potential. This is not a statement of the obvious. Like so many things American, our talent

---

[21]See "Fact and Fancy in Assigning Grades," *Basic College Quarterly,* Winter, 1957, page 11.

hunt has taken the form of a search for numbers, a preoccupation with education for the average many as against the superior few. As a result, we find the intellectually gifted student, particularly in his freshman year, expressing disappointment. The Counseling Center at Michigan State found them saying things like the following:

"I learned a lot this year, but it has not been as challenging as I would like."

"The basic courses are much too easy, although the honor section in course W was a trifle more demanding in terms of quantity of work required. Course L is one of the best, not because it is so challenging, but because it is taught as though each student is expected to do independent thinking. This is in contrast to the spoon-feeding in other courses."

"The first term did not challenge me, so in the second term I carried twenty-two credits. Even this load was not demanding in terms of mental effort, but it took more time than I was willing to give. Since this was not the answer, I went back to eighteen credits in the third term."

"I feel strongly about students being permitted to take courses for which they do not have the background. It hurts them and slows up the rest of us when we are in the same classes."

"There is an anti-intellectual feeling among students. It is a disgrace to be smart, and a person should not use his brains if he has any."

"I was especially challenged by course D, which required real effort on my part and resulted in my being permitted to do honors work."[22]

Acceleration by means of special examination is one way of providing for superior students, and this has been the policy in the Basic College since its beginning. A second, and in some ways a superior method, is enriched programs of work. Such a program was begun in Communication Skills during the academic year 1954-1955 for those scoring sufficiently high on the MSU English Placement Test. Slightly less than five per cent of students in the first term of the course were thus enrolled. Most remained

---

[22]See F. H. DeLisle, D. L. Grummon, D. R. Ross, "The Intellectually Gifted Freshman," *Basic College Quarterly*, Fall, 1956, pages 9-10.

in the "honors sections" during the second term, after which a large number gained credit for the third term by special examination. In the light of the reactions from superior students noted above, evaluations (unsigned) of work in the honors sections are noteworthy. Here are a representative few:

"My participation in a special section of Communication Skills has been the most enriching and beneficial educational experience I have ever had. . . . It is added stimulus to listen intently to, observe, and consider fully the opinions and techniques of your fellow students when you know they possess above average ability in a subject."

"This has been the most enjoyable and profitable course I have taken this term. . . . I hope capable students of later classes will be allowed this experience."

"The most interesting and the most fun of all my classes. It was never boring and always stimulating. Sure, it was a little harder than most of the other sections, but I guess that's what made it so much fun. . . . It is what a college course should be."

"Communication Skills has been my most interesting class during my first term at Michigan State University. To a very large degree, I believe this is due to my being in one of the new honor sections. Where we could have gladly cut other classes, most students wanted to go to Communication Skills."

"As John Crosby has said, 'It is difficult to say much of interest about something that is entirely satisfactory.' That seems to be the only excuse I can find for having so little to say about the Communication Skills honor section. This class has been by far my most challenging and most interesting course of the term."

"I have never enjoyed and learned as much in any single course as I have in the Communication Skills honor section. . . . The things I learned about the various subjects we explored in class are proving and will prove invaluable to me."

"Some may feel that an honor section is not fair. We have Improvement Services for those who have trouble in college work, but there was nothing which excited the more intelligent student to work harder and learn more. The honor students need help too. They need an education that excites and challenges them to higher goals."

The curriculum builder, accustomed to the protestations of student grief and colleague irritation which so frequently accompany work in freshman English, may be moved by the above student reactions to observe that the obvious way to have a successful course is to enroll good students and provide them with competent instructors. Alexander Meiklejohn used to say that the freshman student is one who still expects something to happen to him. This is more than a comment on teachers and curriculum, it is a comment on students as well. Good students cause the necessary things to happen.

chapter 3

NATURAL SCIENCE

*John N. Moore**

Introduction

During the first eight years of the Basic College, students were offered general education science in either of two separate courses: one in Biological Science and one in Physical Science. Each course extended through three quarters and gave nine credits. The courses were taught by staff members of autonomous departments under different department heads, and students had the option of selecting either of the two courses as part of their general education program. The purpose of this chapter is to describe methods followed and results obtained when a decision was reached in 1952 to fuse the two science courses into a single course: Natural Science.

General education at Michigan State started as an experiment in 1944, and the reorganization of the Basic College in 1952 must be looked upon as an extension of the initial experiment. Very few precedents for a single course in the natural sciences existed at the college and university level in the United States. Most commonly the field of science had been presented to general education students in separate courses drawn from the biological sciences and the physical sciences. Though the task of evolving a course that would represent a combination of the best of two existing courses is the scope of this chapter, it is necessary to give brief attention to the two science courses that existed when reorganization of the Basic College was planned.

*Department of Natural Science, Michigan State University, East Lansing, Michigan.

The course in Biological Science, just prior to the reorganization of 1952, was designed to help students interpret man in light of his biological nature, and to accomplish this students studied man in relation to all other living things. Students were expected to know certain fundamental biological principles and to understand the relation of these principles both to themselves as individuals and to society. Work was organized under six topics: (1) Kinds of Living Things, (2) Characteristics Common to All Living Things, (3) Maintenance of the Individual, (4) Maintenance of the Species, (5) Interrelationships, and (6) Biological Evolution. The laboratory program was developed with one objective — to teach the student to think scientifically. The purpose of this concentration was to give him a method of thinking and an attitude useful in his daily life.

Prior to 1952, the other general education science course, Physical Science, integrated various facts of astronomy, chemistry, geology, and physics into a texture with threads of philosophic and historical aspects of science. The course was concerned with three major areas: (1) The growth of man's ideas about the origin and structure of the universe and the solar system; the purpose was to help students perceive the function of observation, classification, and generalization in the development of natural laws. (2) Man's observations of the atmosphere and the structure of the earth; the goal was to explain relationships among physical factors in man's environment. (3) An analysis of the structure of matter; topics included the study of heat, molecular structure of matter, and various forms of energy.

These two courses had undergone numerous changes during their eight years of existence. Some mention of the stages in the evolution of each is necessary to illustrate the outlooks of the separate groups of staff members that later were responsible for formulating a single course in the natural sciences. Throughout its history pedagogical efforts in Biological Science had been pointed directly at the teaching of knowledge, abilities, and attitudes. The faculty always emphasized laboratory work, the lectures being considered means for the treatment of ideas after they were encountered in laboratory classwork. Subject matter was considered in some measure a vehicle for illustrating scientific methodology; and for this reason science teaching in Biological Science laboratories progressed through the following three stages: (1) concentrated attention on observation, description, and classification; (2) experiments and specific poblem-solving situations to test hypotheses; (3) subsequent addition of synthesis of ideas into a coherent system, or theory construction.

In 1944 the Biological Science course was organized to effect direct observation. Students were expected to give primary consideration to observation and description within systems of plants and animals. The experiments were limited to recording and observing, with no tests of hypotheses included. In the second year new experiments on photosynthesis were attempted. In these students used preliminary information and interpretations of demonstrations to formulate hypotheses about relationships of events; the hypotheses were then tested.

A second phase of teaching scientific methodology is apparent in Biological Science laboratory manuals wherein explanations and exemplifications of scientific method were added by reference to the function of experiment, statement of problems, formulation of possible solutions, and experiments to test hypotheses so as to familiarize students with this step-wise approach to science.

A third phase in the teaching of scientific methodology appears in the inclusion of the function of theory in a series of studies of heredity leading students through a logical development of ideas and concept formation. Data were presented and hypotheses requested to synthesize ideas into a single coherent system or theory by means of actual student responses. This, however, was only a representative preview of the third phase, developed more extensively in the second year of Natural Science.

Such a three-phase development did not occur in the first eight years of the Physical Science laboratory program. Laboratories were conducted along the lines of traditional experiments in chemistry and physics, based on quantitative work and calculations of physical interrelationships. Laboratories also involved direct manipulation of material and equipment by students to obtain data through their own efforts at measurement. There was marked emphasis in the early years upon a mathematical orientation to illustrate and verify principles and laws typical of the orderly physical sciences. The lectures aimed at knowledge, skills, and attitudes, with laboratories functioning primarily in a confirmatory manner. There were no attempts to integrate science through a specific, simplified, step-wise process as in the first two phases of Biological Science. No formal work with problems, hypotheses, and tests was incorporated into the Physical Science course.

Student criticism of the emphasis on mathematical orientation and quantification produced a change in 1950 to a course organized around major ideas taken from the history and philosophy of science. Demonstration of classic experiments on falling bodies and development of problem solving in meteorology and geology resulted in the addition of the interpretation and prediction of weather and the classification of rocks. The main approach to theory as an explanatory mechanism was handled in lecture. These changes were made in the belief that the course in Physical Science could not make a permanent contribution of real significance to the educational experiences of students if it had as its main aim the survey of common physical phenomena.

This brief historical review indicates clearly that staff members in Biological Science and in Physical Science had followed different lines of approach to their common task of developing general education science courses. Understandably, when the Dean of the Basic College proposed, in February, 1952, a merger of Physical Science with Biological Science into one department, staff members of the two departments were quite unprepared. Both departments had been so deeply involved in efforts to evolve their own courses that they had had neither time nor inclination to give attention to a change that would amalgamate the two into a single general education science department.

Nevertheless, circumstances required consolidation of the science areas of the Basic College. Student enrollments for 1951-1952 in Physical Science totaled approximately 1500 (about 500 per quarter) compared to over 8200 (about 3000 per quarter) in Biological Science. This differential in enrollments was due in part to upper school curricular requirements which had omitted Physical Science in favor of Biological Science. The disparity in enrollments was one of the factors underlying the decision to merge the two departments.

When given an opportunity in February, 1952, to express an opinion, a majority of Biological Science staff members voted "no" on any immediate plan to reorganize general education science

at Michigan State. This attitude reflected a realistic analysis by
the group of the problems of combining the biological sciences and
the physical sciences; perhaps, too, it was a reflection of the natural
resistance of most human beings to sudden change. The Physical
Science faculty also voted against the proposed reorganization.

At one meeting of the Biological Science staff, after actuality
of course reorganization was recognized, the editor of an early
Laboratory Guide for Biological Science indicated his ideas of what
the suggested course, which might be called "Natural Science,"
should include: Evolution, Biogenesis, Laws of Genetics, Cell
Theory, Concepts of Ecology and Parasitism, Relativity, Quantum
Theory, Atomic Molecular Theory, Laws of Mechanics, Laws of
Optics, Laws of Thermodynamics, and Laws of Electricity. This
was apparently the first step that is so necessary in stimulating
group action. Not many staff members agreed to the inclusion of
all these topics in one course. Even the author of this proposal
expressed pessimism because he could see no unifying principles,
laws, or theories under which the multitudinous details of the
physical sciences and the biological sciences might be subsumed.
Such were some of the activities preceding the first joint meeting
of the Physical Science staff and the Biological Science staff.

Development of the First Course

At the first meeting of the combined staffs the head of the
Department of Biological Science presided. Discussion of the name
of the new course brought out disapproval of the name, "Science,"
and the chairman indicated that he had requested that the new
course be given the more acceptable name of "Natural Science."

In order to elicit ideas regarding curricular content from all
people involved, five sub-committees were formed, each including
four or five biologists and one or two physical scientists. Each
committee was charged with planning, as soon as possible, a course
outline for "Natural Science" for presentation to the "committee as
a whole." An article, entitled "Deriving the Objectives and Content of the College Curriculum: The Natural Sciences," was distributed for discussion at a later date.

The group was asked to consider, "In what ways do we
expect the thousands of students to change as a result of taking
our (the new) course?" Suggested answers were: development

of an interest in and appreciation of science; curiosity, ability to understand themselves and the universe; development of objective thinking, of appreciation of the operation of the scientific method, and the ability to use it; and, finally, understanding of major concepts. When asked, "Which concept would you include if you could take only one?", the biologists immediately responded: evolution. For the physical scientists the answer was the matter-energy concept. These were trial considerations which helped the group find common ground from which to move. There was easy agreement that the Natural Science course would be terminal, and not a specifically planned pre-requisite to upper school science courses. At the close of that first meeting it was agreed that the combined staffs would meet each week, thus making twelve meetings available before conclusion of the academic year at mid-June, 1952.

Initial reports of the sub-committees contained recommendations for a course in (1) interest in and appreciation of science by developing the habit of thinking objectively, (2) study of major unifying principles of science with classical rather than technological emphasis, (3) study of principles by problem approach based on continuity of man's attempt to understand natural phenomena, and (4) study of concepts of order, change, continuity of life, and relationships.

Discussion of each of the schemes brought out further aspects of consensus of the combined staffs. First, it was recognized that laboratory work would be problem centered with students actually handling materials. The group decided that great effort would be exerted to make this possible so as to avoid "dry labs" wherein students talked about the real objects of scientific work and did paper work only. Second, the desirability of continuity throughout the three-quarter sequence of classwork was approved unanimously. One sub-committee wanted to use study of the methods of science as the thread of continuity for the new course. Third, five criteria, which could be used for selecting subject matter, were given serious consideration by the entire group. The criteria were:

(a) General interest, timeliness, student interest
(b) Simplicity of presentation
(c) Permanence (social significance)
(d) Integrative value
(e) Philosophical significance

To develop more concrete understanding of the task at hand among the biologists and physical scientists, each sub-committee was assigned preparation of written reports in answer to the following questions:

1. Why teach general education courses?
2. What part does Natural Science play in general education?
3. What should be the major content of the Natural Science course?

Duplicated copies of answers to these questions by each sub-committee were distributed for study before the regular Friday meeting in the third week in March, 1952. The final reports revealed several areas of agreement in the answers to the first two questions. General education was a means whereby students increased their sensitivity to their environment, formed a frame of reference by which solutions to problems might be worked out, and functioned as a counter-acting measure to specialization in professional and vocational pursuits. Natural Science was offered to help the student become aware of problems arising from his biological nature and physical environment, to develop an interest in and appreciation of science, and to emphasize the orderliness of nature.

As to the content of the Natural Science course, marked divergence of opinion was reflected in four of the final committee reports. The following illustrate the main ideas mentioned in approaching the third question:

1. The content of Natural Science should draw more heavily upon physics for basic information and techniques than upon any other single science. Problems relating to immediate material reward and problems of a non-utilitarian nature involving the search for order and comprehension were listed.

2. The Natural Science course should include content which would meet the needs of students. The new course should move away from the traditional point of view that subject matter should be dictated by the teacher without considering student interests and needs. Emphasis should be given to individual student approach to problems so as to work out, with teacher direction, problem identification, beliefs, expected results, tests, and reports

of actual results. Laboratory procedure would provide maximum student self-direction with teacher guidance, cooperative planning and execution of action.

3. The major content should involve study of the origin of things, the nature of things, and the interactions of organisms with each other and with the environment. Laboratories should emphasize treatment of principles by the problem method.

4. The beginning of Natural Science could be concerned with the unique characteristics of man which have enabled him to develop conceptual thinking with regard to himself and his surroundings. Following this introduction, the subject matter would include the following topics: orderliness of cosmic phenomena, energy relationships, organization of protoplasm, organic evolution, development of living organisms, and ecological patterns.

It was evident that considerable disagreement existed about the kind of laboratory experiences students should have: some staff members took the position that instructors should select the laboratory problems, another group held that students were best motivated if they selected the problems themselves. Proponents of the latter position wanted to give students opportunities for working in groups, to gain experience in self-direction and cooperation. Those who supported this so-called "student-centered" course sought to institute something truly new, almost revolutionary, in mass education science teaching at the college and university level: implementation of a non-authoritarian educational philosophy.

However, most of the staff were traditionally subject-centered instructors who approached the problem of formulating Natural Science in a different way. They saw the natural sciences as so complex that the rather immature student had to be guided to an interest in certain areas where there were no "felt needs." Clearly an impasse had been reached. The department head called for other procedures. One plan suggested a reshuffle of the sub-committees in the hope that new ideas for solving the problem of content would stem from a new juxtaposition of individuals. An alternative suggestion was the appointment of three representatives of each committee as a curriculum committee empowered to map out the course. The second plan was accepted. But, how would decisions be made? The chairman extolled the "Quaker method" wherein all could talk until exhausted or converted.

Such talking did occur, and the subject-matter specialists prevailed over those who supported a student-centered course. In the last week of March, 1952, with Natural Science planned as a "must" for inauguration the succeeding fall, subject matter was allocated on a tentative time basis by topics. Atomic-molecular theory, evolution (with classification), ecological patterns, cycles of elements, and food chains were topics envisaged as warranting from three to four weeks each.

The task, which each staff member faced, of enlarging his knowledge and understanding from the biological sciences exclusively to include the physical sciences, or from the physical sciences exclusively to include the biological sciences, was a trying intellectual struggle. There were several who resolved to have nothing to do with the project and they sought employment at other institutions.

In the short time between winter and spring quarters, some of the "practical" minds developed a comprehensive outline for lecture and laboratory under four headings:

I. Man as a Biological Organism
   A. Characteristics of living organisms
   B. Maintenance of an individual organism

II. The Unique Characteristics of Man
   (Perception as initial act of learning, symbolization, and scientific methodology)

III. Man Looks at His Environment
   A. Matter and energy
   B. Interrelationships of organisms and the physical environment
   C. Interrelationships of organisms and their living environment
   D. The nature of the stellar universe
   E. Origin and geological development of the earth
   F. Organic evolution

IV. Man's Attempts to Control His Environment
   A. Invention and technology
   B. Germ theory of disease

    C. Conservation of natural and human resources

    D. Man's changing concepts of man

Several weeks were spent in revising the proposed outline and resolving specific problems. One area of concern centered on a projected comparison of living and non-living things, the inanimate machine and animate "machine." Such an attempt seemed too analytic, mechanistic, and non-humanistic to many staff members. Their fear of excessive emphasis on the mechanistic concept was allayed by the inclusion of the study of the uniqueness of man.

In discussing the area of matter and energy, the group expressed the opinion that emphasis should be upon development of ideas, not on history. The group was aware of the easy tendency, due to "vested interests," to include as much as possible. At the same time no agreement could be reached on which criterion or set of criteria should be used to effect selection. There was, however, agreement to discard the last section of the outline on man's changing concepts of man as being beyond the scope of a course in the natural sciences.

As a consequence of the pressing deadline, group members accepted the necessary, real conditions they faced and selected some 30 laboratory studies for the first year of Natural Science. They admitted quite unblushingly that the first set of laboratory studies would be inadequate and that the course would not embody the full outline as set out under the main headings; nor would the accepted course rationale be properly implemented. A check of laboratory studies available in laboratory manuals for the old Biological Science and Physical Science courses showed 11 studies which were usable; another 9 studies for which materials were available, but additional work was needed to prepare them for class use, and 10 laboratory assignments for which new material had to be prepared in six weeks.

Consequently staff members selected laboratory studies on which they wished to work. In some instances only one person was involved, but more often two, three, and even four members desired to work on certain studies. These groups were encouraged to work regularly and to write material for the laboratory studies. All were reminded that the emphasis of the Natural Science course would be upon the laboratory work, the sole function of lectures

being to explain and enlarge ideas first encountered by students
in their laboratory experiences. The two-hour laboratory was to
be followed by a one-hour recitation period each week. Two one-
hour lecture periods per week were supplemental to these classes.
Students would receive twelve credits toward graduation upon successful completion of three quarters of Natural Science.

Authors of the laboratory program sought to achieve these
ends: (1) the student was to solve problems by his own processes,
(2) concepts presented were to be of major importance, and (3)
the student was to develop understanding of how discoveries are
made. In regard to the latter point, authors were urged to study
the history of the selected areas to determine the important and
the significant.

The major task of the course was to convey to students what
science is, what science has done, and what the limitations of
science are.

The table of contents of the *Guide for Laboratory Studies*:
Natural Science, published in September, 1952, was as follows:

First Term Work:

1)   The Cell
2)   The Nature of Matter
3)   Diffusion in Living Things
4)   Cellular Respiration
5)   Organ Systems
6)   Foods and Digestion (used only in lectures)
7)   Cells and Internal Environment
8)   The Nervous System and Reflex Behavior
9)   Sensory Perception
10) Measurement (not used)
11) Symbolization
12) The Relation of Symbols

Second Term Work:

13) Motion of a Freely Falling Body
14) Temperature and Quantity of Heat
15) Heat
16) The Periodic Law
17) Light and Color

18) Photosynthesis
19) Biological and Physical Cycles in Nature
20) The Influence of Organisms on Their Environment
21) Weather

Third Term Work:
22) Populations and Heredity I
23) Populations and Heredity II
24) Populations and Heredity III
25) Populations and Heredity IV
26) Kinds of Living Things: Animal
27) Kinds of Living Things: Plants
28) Rocks and Fossils
29) Skeletal Homology
30) Some Evidence of Evolution
31) Classification of Man

Before final copy of the laboratory guide was approved, staff members gave serious consideration to the question of a textbook or textbooks. Several texts in physical science and biology and general works on the development of science had been studied while the laboratory program was under discussion. Among these were Cohen, *Science, Servant of Man;* Lemon, *Physical Science;* Cheronis, *Study of the Physical World;* and Pauli, *The World of Life.* The staff realized that no one book existed which would serve as *the* textbook in Natural Science. Though no integrating principles had been found, and their discovery was not even expected for the first year, the group sought some unification of the new course. The great hope was to avoid separation of subject matter into one quarter of chemistry and physics, a second quarter of botany and zoology, and a third quarter of geology.

To solve the problem of the lack of an adequate textbook in Natural Science in an expedient manner, appropriate sections from the *Biological Science Lecture Syllabus* and the *Physical Science Lecture Syllabus* were assembled into a combined syllabus. The combined syllabus was prepared as a stop gap for use during the first year only. Some staff members voiced objection that the combined syllabus for Natural Science was not well integrated and should only be an outline supplement to two textbooks. But a majority voted in favor of the combined syllabus as a guide for lectures in Natural Science.

During preparation of the first Natural Science course the whole group acted on all problems. All members had opportunities through sub-committees and plenary meetings of the combined staffs to contribute to solutions of the numerous problems faced. Undoubtedly this *modus operandi* was painstaking and time consuming; yet the procedure facilitated communication among people from widely diverse academic backgrounds, and had the added benefit of involving the maximum number of persons in construction of the course.

Active Discussion of Revision

The group activity of proposal and counter-proposal, outline and counter-outline during those momentous months from February into June evolved a consensus against a thin survey of physical and biological topics. The next Natural Science course would involve a program that penetrated several ideas: a true block and gap curricular design. The course would develop around major ideas of the cell, evolution, mechanics, the particle, and possibly relativity. Methods of science would serve as the integrating medium. The group approved, in general terms, such a projected revision of Natural Science even before a single class had convened; and it was recommended that everyone begin reading background and resource materials. The development of science and its relation to society would be the backbone of the second course in Natural Science.

Thus weaknesses in the first course, the product of expediency, were recognized. The short range goal of a set of classroom exercises for 1952-1953 had been attained in the limited time of four months. Yet dissatisfaction with the lecture syllabus and with the laboratory guide was expressed openly, for many members of the department realized that adequate criteria for selection of course content had not been developed. That too much had been included in the first Natural Science course is obvious from the table of contents of the *Guide for Laboratory Studies: Natural Science,* above.

In a search for a fresh approach to curriculum planning, staff members attempted to discover students' understanding and beliefs about problems and questions in science when they began the course. To accomplish this, a pretest or questionnaire was administered for several weeks during the fall quarter, 1952. Students in randomly selected classes were asked to state their beliefs as answers to questions related to topics of the first quarter. In dicussing the questionnaires the department head emphasized that it was necessary to begin a course in general education science where the student was. The questionnaire was a simple device through which the staff could ascertain the general level of student science comprehension. The project was expanded during the first year of Natural Science to include questions associated with topics of the second and third quarters of the course. Results of all the questionnaires were made available to those engaged in revising the laboratory work.

By the third staff meeting of the newly constituted Department of Natural Science, staff members were actively discussing the projected revision for 1953-54. Early discussion centered around three areas: Reproduction and Heredity, Photosynthesis and Respiration Relationships, and Cosmology. However, it was agreed that nothing was fixed and change could be gradual or complete. That the design of classwork was to be developed according to the Biological Science laboratory approach was accepted as a mandate for all authors participating in the revision. This meant that all three phases of implementing the teaching of scientific methodology, alluded to briefly at the beginning of this chapter, would be developed further in the second year of Natural Science. Staff members also supported the idea of a book containing both laboratory exercises and closely integrated textual matter rather than separate publications of each. However, continued emphasis on laboratory work left no time for the preparation of textual material during the first revision of Natural Science.

Direction of course revision was not the responsibility of the "committee as a whole." Primarily because of increase in staff size, a new division of labor was devised for the first revision. As a modification of large group activity, a six-member Curriculum Committee was appointed by the department head to direct the new project. He made clear the degree of delegation of responsibility for planning and writing. Development of new and revised material for each quarter was assigned to three separate sub-committees appointed from membership of the Curriculum Committee.

Reports of sub-committees of the Curriculum Committee indicated that the first quarter would cover reproduction and heredity; the second quarter would deal with matter and energy, centered on the particle, with photosynthesis and metabolism as extensions; and the third quarter would include the changing aspects of the earth and organic evolution. It became apparent that a successful course organization in Natural Science was contingent on full exploitation of empirical and theoretical aspects of scientific methodologies as the unifying theme throughout the three quarters of the course.

Very important to the search for ways of developing methodology as the unifying scheme were discussions of Conant, *Science and Common Sense*. The group spent several meetings in serious study of that book as a text for the next year. After lengthy argument a close vote showed the staff in favor of Conant and two textbooks as supplements to a laboratory manual. Ideas contained in Conant were to be used as material for examinations and in writing laboratory exercises. These decisions demonstrated clearly an intention to increase the emphasis on conceptual and theoretical aspects of scientific activity in the course; and these decisions reflected, too, the influence of subject matter specialists who had continually wanted to use reference texts. This opinion was supported by teaching experiences in the first quarter wherein inadequacies of the *Natural Science Lecture Syllabus* were most evident. Others held, however, that such a set of textbooks would surely enlarge the risk of separateness of subject matter, and weaken the integrative function of scientific method as the common theme of the three quarters of classwork.

During the winter quarter textbook selection occupied the Curriculum Committee; sub-committees preparing materials for each quarter reported to the staff. Frequent seminars were held. One seminar was devoted to presentation of student reactions to Biological Science and Physical Science. Another seminar dealt with the methodologies of science and was particularly important in developing staff consensus and aiding authors of laboratory studies.

In February, 1953, the Curriculum Committee announced selection of Krauskopf, *Fundamentals of Physical Science;* Hardin,

Biology, Its Human Implications; and Conant, *Science and Common Sense* as supplemental textbooks and reference aids for student work in the staff-prepared laboratory guide.

The physical science textbook was chosen (1) because of its treatment of such fields as astronomy, mechanics, chemistry, electricity, geology, and atomic-nuclear physics, and (2) because of the author's repeated attention to types of indirect and direct evidences of scientific phenomena, including good historical background of modern day concepts. The biological science textbook is generally descriptive, but was chosen because it makes science "an intellectual adventure!" Basic principles are used to point up methodology of science, and scientific method and historical material are used as means for presenting research in each of the subject areas of the textbook.

Conant is an expanded publication of *On Understanding Science,* in which Dr. Conant entertains such questions as "What is science?" What are conceptual schemes?" "What is the relationship of science to politics, and the relationship of science to world events?" This book was significant for students and lecturers because of the great emphasis placed upon the analysis of scientific methods of experimental inquiry, quantitative experimentation, the development of the chemical revolution, the concept of spontaneous generation, uniformitarianism, and the relationships of science to industry, medicine, and the state. Through selected case histories of research into scientific phenomena, it aided the attainment of two main objectives of the course: study of scientific methodology and treatment of the social implications of scientific work.

After editing and approving each laboratory study the Curriculum Committee distributed duplicated copies to the staff for comments and criticisms. As publication deadline approached, the Curriculum Committee was forced to abandon a plan to publish materials in one binding in favor of a more flexible publication arrangement. Therefore the new laboratory exercises were published in three volumes called *Studies in Natural Science.* Writing for the revised Natural Science course was influenced by teaching experience gained in the early part of the first year; one noticeable characteristic of the new volumes was the liberal reference to Conant throughout.

The table of contents for the *Studies in Natural Science* series included:

Volume One

Introduction — A Word to the Student

1. Perception and Symbolization
2. Sexual Reproduction
3. The Cell Theory
4. Cellular Respiration
     Panel Discussion Directions
5. Heredity I
     A Student Project in Human Heredity
6. Heredity II
7. Heredity III
8. Heredity IV
9. Heredity V
10. Heredity VI

Classwork began with attention to man's methods of representing objects and events in symbolic manner. After this first exercise, the next three directed the student's attention to gross observation of organs and cells involved in sexual reproduction and to the study of life activities of cells in general. The series on heredity elicited hypotheses and required repeated examination of the method employed throughout the development of the six studies. Each study provided more data to be explained by the particulate theory of the gene. Thus by means of assumptions or postulates stated and hypotheses developed, the students experienced a process of theory formulation as they synthesized ideas into a coherent system. The last part of the series also included reference to Lysenko's genetics and the social implications of scientific doctrine developed in the Russian totalitarian state.

Volume Two

11. Physical and Chemical Changes
12. The Gas Laws
13. The Kinetic Theory

14. The Theory of the Atom
15. Electricity and the Nature of Matter
16. Transformation of Solar Energy
17. Cellular Respiration
18. Cells and the Internal Environment (Appendix — never used in Natural Science)

Volume Two required quantification work in which students dealt with collected data, analyzed results for possible relationships by algebraic and graphic means, and then tested the fitness of traditional gas laws to the data collected and analyzed. Students studied assumptions of the Kinetic Theory and the atomic theory to explain states of matter and changes in states of matter. Another feature of Volume. Two was a specially prepared three-week historical case study of electricity involving descriptions, problem solving, and synthesis of conceptualizations. Quotations from Gilbert, von Guericke, DuFay, Franklin, Oersted, Rowland, Rutherford, Thomson, and Bohr were presented in separate sections to add more data, thus leading toward the modern concept of the atom with nucleus and surrounding parts. Where possible the materials and apparatus involved were available for student use and study.

Volume Three
General Introduction

19. Minerals
20. Rocks
21. Changes in Land Features I
22. Changes in Land Features II
23. Animal Relationships
24. Populations and the Mechanisms of Organic Evolution
25. Evidences of Evolution
26. Experimental Evolution
27. Evolution, Genetics, and the Races of Man

Volume Three was primarily descriptive and classificatory, dealing with minerals, rocks, and land features of the earth's sur-

face and with classification of animals. Theories of rock formation were discussed. It included also population mechanics, graphs,
and generalizations stemming from genetic mechanisms in evolution. By means of the data presented, problem-solving situations
were evolved that led to extension of the gene theory as it might
be related to the theory of natural selection. The experimental
evolution study involved utilization and explanation of data to
enlarge upon the usefulness of natural selection as a mechanism in
organic evolution. The final study provided for the application
of postulates of population dynamics and genetic mechanism to
classification of man.

In the 1953 series, one finds concerted emphasis on implementation of theory construction. From this time students studied
theory construction as an aspect of scientific methodology that goes
beyond the previously developed processes of description, classification, and problem solving; the latter involved observation, statement of a problem, hypothesis formulation, and tests of hypotheses.
However, the area of theory construction was still embryonic in
the 1953 series and pedagogical techniques for handling the work
were in some places quite halting, incomplete, and unsuccessful.

During the year, discussions devoted to preparation and review of revised materials were characterized by close votes repeatedly.
There still were several dissenters to the whole effort to develop
a course in general education science emphasizing selected areas of
the natural sciences. This probably was good for a general atmosphere of check and counter-check, and it contributed to a balance
of interests within the whole staff. Nevertheless, the reluctance of
some persons to participate as authors placed the actual work of
revision on fewer shoulders. From the point of view of efficiency
of operation, this was advantageous: fewer individual outlooks had
to be reconciled in preparing the finished product.

New Curriculum Committee, New Revision

Staff efforts for reduction and modification of course content
were evident in the academic year of 1953-1954 while the revised
Studies in Natural Science volumes were used along with two textbooks and a reference book. Defects in the laboratory studies,
detected early in the fall quarter, prompted the department head to
appoint a new Curriculum Committee. Responsibility for collect-

ing criticisms and planning a second revision of Natural Science was delegated to the new eight-member committee.

Staff meeting notes of that year reveal that the entire staff was busy with numerous details, such as further development of lectures, problems dealing with development of suitable examinations, and handling of royalties from the sale of staff-prepared books.

Near the close of the spring quarter, 1954, staff members considered several proposals from the Curriculum Committee; first among these was a motion to reverse the order of the second and third quarters of the course. The second quarter material of gas laws, molecular phenomena, electricity, and atomic theory was regarded as most abstract in nature; therefore, the Curriculum Committee recommended that discussion of such physical science topics was more fitting for students who had completed two quarters of university work. This recommendation seemed doubly wise because of the theoretical scientific methods involved in that type of knowledge. The general framework of the course which was recommended was as follows: first quarter, Reproduction and Heredity; second quarter, Geology and Organic Evolution; and third quarter, Atomic-Molecular Theory and Electricity. The staff gave unanimous approval to the proposal. The sequence of volumes of the *Studies in Natural Science* series was changed accordingly for the year 1954-1955.

A second proposal of the Curriculum Committee, that students should continue to use books by Hardin, Krauskopf, and Conant in 1954-1955, was also given unanimous approval. Teaching and testing were better as a result of experience in the use of these materials in the then current year.

The Curriculum Committee also recommended that "a combination of textual material and laboratory exercises should be prepared by staff members as a 1955-1956 revision of the Natural Science course. Textual material should appear in two columns per page for easy eye span with good quality paper employed to guarantee reproduction of illustrations. Problem solving would not be lost because examples representing the laboratory material should be used [in the text chapters], hence providing students with an opportunity to check answers to laboratory problems. Such a text-laboratory book should give unity, coherence, and meaning to ideas developed; lecture, recitation and laboratory procedures could be conducted as a unit." There was much discussion of this proposal. Though the three books mentioned above were to be used during 1954-1955, the majority recognized that a book written by staff members was required. Even those who had criticized the *Natural Science Lecture Syllabus* were convinced that a combined text-laboratory book would strengthen the teaching of Natural Science. There was unanimous approval of the proposal.

The year 1953-1954 witnessed lengthy consideration of the terminology used in describing the methods of scientists. By means of regular seminars, the staff achieved understanding and agreement concerning the use of terminology. The group accepted unanimously the conclusion that there was no routine, uniform scientific method comprised of several artificially identified "steps." Rather, staff members preferred the view that numerous single and compound methods of scientists are employed both in the laboratory and in contemplation.

Late in the second year of Natural Science much time was also spent in careful consideration of outlines for each quarter prepared by Curriculum Committee members and by individual staff members. Discussion of two outlines for the first quarter pointed up these questions: (1) Are students interested in reproduction but not in the cell? (2) Should the cell theory be set within some general problem? (3) Should material still be selected to illustrate scientific methods, impact of subject matter, and significance of subject matter? (4) Should the course begin with a study of the process of symbolization? Altogether, fifteen subtitles were suggested for the first quarter, and only one clear decision was reached when a majority responded in the affirmative to the last question.

The only difference in three outlines presented for the second quarter was the inclusion of topics on weather and climate in one of them. A straw vote indicated that staff members did not favor such an inclusion. There was a somewhat closer consensus on geology and organic evolution, for only six different sub-titles were proposed.

Four tentative outlines for the third quarter were circulated and discussed in June, 1954. At that time opinions were registered that (1) too much time had been allotted the atomic theory, (2) students were more interested in atomic energy than in historical analysis of the development of the concepts involved, and (3) it would be very difficult to devote laboratory time to a consideration of the concept of energy. Actually, down to the present time, derivation of course work in the third quarter areas has been most difficult for the Natural Science staff. Only within the past few years have members been added to the staff who have had special experience in general education teaching of the physical sciences. The difficulty of attracting physicists, chemists, and mathematicians to general education teaching has been perennial since the inception of the Basic College. With the arrival of such trained and experienced personnel and the slow gain in command of physical science concepts by biologists originally in the Biological Science department, the third quarter approximates a degree of integration previously characteristic of the other two quarters.

The close of spring quarter, 1954, arrived with no precise plan for revision of Natural Science. One might say that the Curriculum Committee had spent the entire year in search of still elusive criteria to replace "vested interests" in determining the subject matter content of the course. At this point the department head proposed a way to reconcile the outlines: "Let us have one outline which permits variation. We aim to develop intellectual appreciations of the student in science. The cell is the basic concept in the first quarter, uniformitarianism and evolution in the second quarter, and the particle and atomic-molecular theory in the third quarter. The core theme should be: understanding science in terms of what it can contribute to the student in solving human problems, understanding the part of science in working out problems of the universe and man. Different approaches may be used in different quarters or more than one approach in any one quarter."[1] Staff members gave these ideas unanimous approval. The tentative outline was divided into 10 areas, and volunteers indicated their desire to read, study, and write about them. They were: introduction to science, cell theory, germ theory, reproduction, heredity, geology,

---

[1] A more complete statement of the rationale of the present course may be found in "Natural Science" by Chester A. Lawson, *The Basic College of Michigan State*, edited by Thomas Hamilton and Edward Blackman, Michigan State University Press, 1955, pp. 50-53.

evolution, early atomic theory, electricity and magnetism, and modern atomic theory. Thus a general plan for individual study in the summer months of 1954 was laid out quite clearly.

Continued Work on Revision

The year of 1954-1955 was a period of consolidation and critical analysis. Once again staff members considered possible content material for each quarter. Teaching experience in areas of the first quarter and library research persuaded the staff to (1) retain an initial study on perception and symbolization, (2) place sexual reproduction after some descriptive work on cells and tissues, and (3) eliminate cellular respiration from the laboratory work. Some members proposed that the treatment of heredity should be condensed; many felt that the subject could be taught in four weeks with certain minor deletions. However, the full set of six studies was retained because of completeness of presentation of the gene theory. Brief discussion of topics on the solar system and physical aspects of the earth was proposed as a natural prelude to the study of minerals and rocks in the outline for the second quarter. No other suggestions were presented, and the outline was accepted quickly as essentially that which had been taught during the previous year.

In opening discussion on a proposed outline for the third quarter, the department head indicated that he did not know yet whether work should be restricted to the particle concept, or whether energy relations should be included too. Many staff members expressed the opinion that quantitative aspects of methods in physical science should be included. One physical scientist explained that quantitative handling of material meant student collection of data by means of his own measurements of objects or phenomena. The department head urged caution in this direction to avoid some mistakes of authors of the early Physical Science course. The majority favored a "middle ground" plan for treatment of quantitative methods — that is, neither quantitative treatment all through the term, nor none at all. A limiting factor was a budgetary one: funds available determined the amount and kind of physical science teaching equipment that could be purchased.

Late in the fall quarter, 1954, an announcement that the deadline for publication of revised material had been set for April

30, 1955, stimulated immediate discussion about the use of the three volume series of *Studies in Natural Science* for another year. Such action would gain another twelve months' time for preparation of the combined text-laboratory publication. However, staff members were in favor of completing the project for the next school year. The department head, as editor, set a manuscript deadline of February 1, 1955. This would permit the authors three months' writing time and allow another three months for editing.

To get on with definite assignments, outlines for the three quarters were placed on a blackboard and staff members indicated their first and second choices. The final outcome showed a total of 33 staff members involved as primary or collateral authors for the new revision. The editor suggested that all authors working on material for a particular term would need to cooperate closely. From that suggestion developed the plan for authors of material for each quarter to meet as committees, with the editor serving *ex officio*. In this way the over-all course structure would be made clear. Each author was instructed to write as an individual, with frequent checks with others in the appropriate group. Each author was further instructed to write textual material to accompany each laboratory study. The editor indicated that this design would insure that textual material preceding one study would be tied in adequately with the previous study or textual matter.

Work proceeded well throughout the winter and spring quarters of that year. However, material for the last two-thirds of the new revision did not reach the editor as rapidly as he had anticipated. Therefore, instead of publishing the new material in one volume, it became necessary to prepare three volumes of textual and laboratory material in combination. This change guaranteed the availability of at least the first quarter material for fall quarter classes in 1955. There was the added advantage of greater flexibility in time for preparation of the other two volumes. Nevertheless, the third volume in the new series did not materialize on schedule. The same old nemesis of what to include in the particle-atomic-molecular theory area of Natural Science resulted in repeated delays. Not until one full year after the originally scheduled publication did *Natural Science*, Volume Three, reach the classroom. This necessitated continued use of *Studies in Natural Science*, Volume Two, until April, 1957.

Another problem faced the Natural Science staff during preparation of the second revision of the course: How to give credit to authors of each section? Since staff members had written textual material as well as laboratory exercises, the long standing policy of anonymous authorship for departmental publications was scrutinized anew. Ever since the formulation of the Basic College, the general policy had been simply to list as contributors the names of staff members in an alphabetical manner near the title page of each publication. In 1954 the Natural Science staff had voted to have the author's name appear with his chapter. By the time a manuscript for the first quarter was written, several difficulties had arisen which militated against easy fulfillment of the newer policy. For one thing, authors of the second revision had used many parts and sections from previous editions. Also, double authorship had been reduced to single authorship in some cases. A scheme was proposed whereby the name of each staff member would be listed after the numbered chapters in which he had participated. However, this plan was not adopted because of the extended history of authorship and revision of material used in the Natural Science course. Most of the exercises were traceable to very early publications of the Biological Science and Physical Science departments. When all factors had been considered, the consensus of staff members was that one alphabetical list of all department members at the time of publication should appear in each volume.

Such has been the development of the course in Natural Science and the preparation of special classroom materials for a general education science course required of all students attending Michigan State University. The first two volumes of the present series are fully designed as combination textbook and laboratory manual publications. The third volume still does not represent a complete combination of text material and laboratory exercises. Students are required to utilize *Fundamentals of Physical Science* as a textbook in the third quarter.

Many more topics might be included at this point in a chapter written to tell the story of how the present course in Natural Science developed. Also, topics associated with unsolved problems which loom big for the future might be outlined. Some of these would involve discussion of constant change and clarification of ideals, development of proper proportion of theory and practice, attempts to develop better reasoning ability in students, and education of staff members in fields other than their own specialty. However, such topics fall beyond the scope of this chapter. At this point a brief review of the present Natural Science course is presented.

Present Course Organization

The table of contents of *Natural Science*, Volume One, is as follows:

Introduction — A Word to the Student

Area I.   Methods of Science
*Chapter   1. Observation, Symbolization and the Method of Empiricism
Chapter   2. Perception and the Methods of Science

Area II.   The Cell
*Chapter   3. Cells, Their Structure and Function
Chapter   4. Organization of Knowledge of the Cell
Chapter   5. The Historical Origin of the Modern Concept of the Cell

Area III. Reproduction
Chapter   6. The Function of Experiment in the Clarification of Ideas Concerning Spontaneous Generation
*Chapter   7. Sexual Reproduction
Chapter   8. Reproduction in Animals and Plants
Chapter   9. Human Reproduction and Sex Hormones
*Chapter 10. Observations on Cellular Reproduction
Chapter   11. Mitosis: Cellular Reproduction

Area IV.   Heredity
*Chapter 12. The Gene Concept and Meiosis
Chapter   13. Genes, Chromosomes and the Nature of a Scientific Theory
*Chapter 14. The Function of the Hypothesized Gene in Explaining Single-Factor Crosses
Chapter   15. The Development of the Gene Concept in Relation to Single-Factor Crosses
*Chapter 16. The Function of the Hypothesized Gene in Explaining Two-Factor Crosses

*Indicates chapters devoted to laboratory exercises.

Of particular note in volume one is the pair of new chapters on observation, symbolization, and empiricism. They set the background for the methodological approaches and emphases employed throughout the three volume series. Following the description of cells and tissues is an entirely new chapter on the historical development of the cell concept. An analysis of the limitations of words in concept building is given extended treatment. Following this is another new chapter on the function of experiment in the work of Redi, Spallanzani, Pouchet, Pasteur, and Tyndall in their attempts to clarify ideas about spontaneous generation. This chapter is primarily a historical treatment of the subject and serves as a foundation for the student's subsequent study of reproductive phenomena. The chapters on reproduction are notably observational and descriptive in nature, but do include an excellent example of method as applied in hormone investigations. The author's discussion follows the line of observation, hypothesis, test, and formulation of new hypotheses.

Closing the first volume is an enlarged series of twelve chapters on heredity. These chapters include emphasis on the hypothesized gene as a particle, postulates, and the relation of postulated behavior of genes and the observed behavior of chromosomes. Emphasis is also given to comparison of expected and actual results, interpretation of data, predictions, and theory construction in the way postulates or assumptions are put together in a synthesis to explain the observable phenomena of inheritance of particular characteritsics in various animals, plants, and human beings. The chapters show the application of the gene theory to the understanding of human beings. A discussion of the social implications of the scientific theory of Lysenko in Russia presents possible impacts of scientific work.

The table of contents of *Natural Science,* Volume Two, includes:

*Indicates chapters devoted to laboratory exercises.

The second volume begins with a new chapter intended to reclarify for the student the accepted meanings of such terms as fact, law, theory, and explanation as they are employed in Natural Science. There follows a series of eleven chapters that are primarily descriptive, and deal with classification of minerals, rocks, and land features of the earth's surface. Some use is made of theory in attempting to explain possible rock origins and, in turn, representative land features. Emphasis on description of animals, plants, and races of man appears in the last half of the second volume. Only where generalizations and deductions concerning the Theory of Natural Selection and extensions of the gene theory are worked out is the student carried beyond the level of empirical enumeration.

By and large the second volume does not present any great improvement over previous material, and handles in only a limited way the problem of theory construction and analysis of the scientific methodology involved. The greatest emphasis in this volume is still upon observation and description. In hindsight, it may be said that this is another example of scientists operating as science educators who handle material primarily in the way of description.

The table of contents of *Natural Science*, Volume Three, contains the following chapter titles:

*Indicates chapters devoted to laboratory exercises.

The first chapter of Volume Three contains something new, the inclusion of aspects of the number concept and problems in the solution of mathematical operations. This material is representative of the quantitative work required of the student throughout the last quarter. An attempt has been made to review quantitative operations important in chosen areas of physical science at a level beyond that found in some high school classrooms. Student attention is directed to assumptions, basic nature of symbol operations, and improvement of proficiency in basic skills not in use in everyday activities.

Following the section on mathematics, quantitative descriptions and definitions of properties of matter, including mass, density, pressure, atmospheric pressure, and temperature, basic to the subsequent study of gas laws, are worked out by simple experiment. Students are also led through the development of symbolic representations of new relations of variables by means commonly handled in mathematics. To give special attention to historical treatment of some tactics and strategy of science in work with gases and pressures, one chapter from *On Understanding Science* by Conant is included to augment the textbook at this point.

New questions calling for interpretation of changes of state and other applications of Kinetic Theory were added to the previously developed study on Kinetic Theory. These serve to demonstrate the usefulness of scientific theory in providing bases for extended explanations. In a similar fashion problems were included after the study on atomic theory, developed in a previous volume, which provided opportunities for application of laws on conservation of matter, definite proportions, and Avogadro's hypothesis. Also, a second chapter from Conant was included after the atomic theory because of his historical treatment of the concept of combustion. This shows the role of experiment, chance discovery, and development of one theory within the sphere of influence of another theory.

In the last area, a modified treatment of static electricity is accomplished through a few changes in the use of pith ball experi-

ments.   A few simple experiments on magnets have been included
to demonstrate some other aspects of the concept of attraction, used
throughout the volume in attempting explanations of physical
phenomena.   Following this experimental work is a chapter on historical references to magnetism and static electricity.   This material,
in much the same form, was originally included in the laboratory
exercises in *Studies in Natural Science,* Volume Two.   It is followed
by a series of questions calling upon the student to analyze the
ways in which concepts of Gilbert, Du Fay, and Franklin were
interwoven in the history of this field.   Classwork in Natural
Science closes with application of postulates of Du Fay and Franklin
to explain the pith ball experiment; then follows a study of experiments supporting synthesis of the particulate concept of current
electricity and leading to the conceptualization of the atom of
Bohr.

Basis Laid for Future Changes

The development of the present course in Natural Science has
come about through contributions of originality and creativity,
research and analysis, and long trial and error of many staff members under the leadership of the department head.   Of particular
importance to future refinements of Natural Science is the continued
stimulus felt by all staff members stemming from research and
analysis by the department head.   Indeed, as the number of staff
members continues to increase, any continued development of the
Natural Science course has become more and more dependent upon
the department head.   Moreover, such conditions contribute to
increased difficulty of communication.   No longer are staff members able to sit around a large conference table and go about the
business of "thrashing out" solutions to mutual problems.

During the year 1954-1955, while staff members were concentrating their energies primarily on the preparation of manu-
scripts for the publications just described, the department head was
seriously involved in an examination of the ways in which scientists
do their work.   His earlier research in cultural evolution had led
him to consider some means of formalizing the analysis of idea
exchange and idea modification.

He had at his disposal several tape recordings of group discussions of staff members.   By application of symbolic logic he was

able to identify certain patterns of idea formulation. He was also able to formalize the dependency of one idea upon another in such representative areas as (1) research by scientists in synthesis of the gene theory and modern day concepts on combustion, (2) development of fundamental ideas in the Protestant Reformation, and (3) organization of the Constitution of the United States and the formulation of democratic government. The fruitfulness of this research became basic to the consideration of even more specific questions, such as, What are the relationships of idea formation to psychologies of learning? Might the mind and body continuum be considered in a new light?

He continued this research through the year of 1955-1956.[2] By the spring of 1956 he realized that the analysis had brought him to some new ways of looking at scientific methodology. He invited a group of staff members to meet during the last quarter of 1956 for the purpose of investigating various ways in which logic might be applied to analyzing the method by which selected theories had been formulated in scientific fields. Members of this logic seminar were excited by the discovery that through analysis of the original work of such men as Newton, Darwin, Dalton and others, a definite pattern of organization in theory formulation could be established.

The group found that identification of borrowed terms, statement of postulates, statement of operations or relationships of terms, definition of invented terms, and deduction of consequences of postulates as new theorems led to clarification of the way in which a particular theory was formulated. Such an analysis also shed light on the essential elements and background necessary before any theory could be understood adequately by instructors and students alike. An apparent outcome of the application of logic to the formation of scientific theories is the establishment of possible criteria of a highly objective nature for subject matter selection. On the basis of the research described it is possible to take any scientific theory and analyze it for borrowed terms, postulates, invented terms, redefinitions, and theorems.

---

[2]The results of this research by the department head, Professor Chester A. Lawson, have been published by the Michigan State University Press: *Language, Thought, and the Human Mind,* 1958.

This new taxonomic, logical-like framework provides a different way of discussing methodology in science. Always there has been too much material in the Natural Science course. Always there has been a pressing need for a set of criteria that could be used in a definitive and objective manner to select course content. At the present stage of the development of this technique of analysis, it seems reasonable to assert that the taxonomic, logical-like framework will provide a means for teaching only those ideas necessary to understanding the terms, postulates, invented terms, redefinitions, and theorems of any particular theory which is selected as typical of work done in representative natural sciences. Of course that amount of observation, description, classification, and experiment which is necessary for grasping ideas basic to any theory would perforce be included in the Natural Science course when the theories have been selected. At the present writing plans are in the formative stage; staff members are engaged in a new revision of Natural Science. Some staff members anticipate that a semi-deductive scheme plus a taxonomic handling of ideas will be generative of a new course organization, one that will stimulate closer integration of the three phases of scientific methodology recognized earlier in this chapter, namely, descriptive, experimental, and theory construction. Some staff members are not convinced that such an approach will be desirable.

Another outcome of this taxonomic, logical-like approach to curriculum change is a new correlation, into the main stream, of research by other staff members. The taxonomic-deductive system is a means for identifying minimum essentials. Minimum essentials of the biological sciences have been the subject of one doctoral dissertation. Undoubtedly there is a reasonable avenue for establishing standards for grading systems based on student command of elements of the taxonomic, logical-like framework. Also there is added need for consideration of the psychological basis of scientific methodology. New attention may be given to scientific attitudes, interests, and motivations of students through the use of beliefs about terms and relationships of ideas held by students as they enter each quarter of the course. It seems altogether reasonable to utilize student beliefs about motion, life, origins of life, creation, etc. as "interest stimulators" during study in a course in Natural Science.

chapter 4

SOCIAL SCIENCE

Douglas Dunham*

The term "Social Science" has been loosely used in the field of general education. Therefore, a description of the processes through which a course by this name has been constructed at Michigan State would seem to require that the title of the course be defined. No doubt there are many equally valid definitions. But as used at Michigan State, the term Social Science has come to mean "an organization and integration of various disciplines concerned with understanding the different aspects of the social behavior of human beings in contemporary society." This is of course a broad definition. There is a danger of construing the definition to mean a complete across-the-board coverage of *all* aspects of human behavior. However, this is not the case, for such a treatment is not only impractical but also unnecessary. Such general coverage would require a vast proliferation of materials that could end only in meaningless confusion. Thus practical considerations as well as intellectual judgment require some selectivity in taking the various disciplines which comprise the social sciences and constructing a unified and meaningful course.

The problem of selectivity immediately poses a value judgment for those who would develop such a course. What disciplines and what areas of human behavior should be included? What left out? At Michigan State, data traditionally organized into the subject matter areas of anthropology, sociology, political science,

---
*Department of Social Science, Michigan State University, East Lansing, Michigan.

economics, and social psychology have formed the core of the materials used. History has been used sparingly, perhaps because a historically oriented course in the Humanities is also required of the same students who take the Social Science course.

But how does a departmental faculty arrive at such a decision? One of the first questions that needs to be answered before even attempting to build the subject matter content of a general education social science course is, what are you trying to do? The position taken, whatever it is, significantly affects the whole orientation of the course. This involves the problem of objectives of such a course. Obviously no course in general education starts out into completely unmarked frontiers. Some guide markers are immediately available.   In planning a curriculum in Social Science, certain University patterns of long standing or faculty or administrative decisions may be assumed as a starting point.   Certain guide posts may be taken as "given": the philosophy of the institution, the philosophy of general education, operational factors in the University, the resources available for learning situations, the attitude of administrators towards curriculum building, the nature of the student body, the experiences and competencies of the available staff. Needless to say, these points vary from one institution to another but at all institutions these and other "given" factors present the operational frame of reference within which the course in Social Science must operate. Thus the fact that Michigan State is on a quarter system rather than a semester plan; that the credit hours for the course were established by faculty action to total first nine term hours, and, after the reorganization of the Basic College, twelve term hours; that each term represents approximately 40 class meetings; that the typical class is of 50 minutes duration; that the instructor can expect to find a wide range of abilities and interest in the student body — these and many others are illustrative of the environment in which the Social Science course was developed.*   A guide line which is not likely to occur elsewhere, though reorganization of courses is a common phenomenon at most institutions, was present when the existing Social Science course was constructed at Michigan State. This resulted from the neces-

---

*For further treatment of the establishment of the Basic College at Michigan State University, see, Hamilton and Blackman (Eds.), *The Basic College at Michigan State*, East Lansing, Michigan State College Press, 1954.

sity of merging the Effective Living course, which was one of the original general education courses established with the Basic College in 1944, and the original Social Science course established at the same time. The two courses were joined in a general reorganization of the Basic College in 1952.

The Effective Living course was the last of the seven Basic College courses developed from the original plans in 1944. Six departments had been established.* A faculty questionnaire distributed throughout the University asked what areas had been omitted for which the faculty might feel there was a need. A variety of responses indicated that such areas as the role of the citizen in the community; individual problems of personality development, health, recreation, family living, and the like had not been specifically included in any of the then proposed six basic courses. The outcome of this thinking was the establishment of a seventh general education course entitled "Effective Living." When this department was subsequently merged with the Social Science Department, the then existing Social Science course needed extensive modification to include part of the content of the Effective Living course. However, since similar problems will hardly occur at other institutions because general education programs are all somewhat different, details of the construction of the Effective Living Department need be presented only in so far as they reflect the guide lines thus set down for the new Social Science course resulting from the merger of Social Science and Effective Living.

The Effective Living course was premised on the assumption that the areas treated would not necessarily be oriented toward meeting requirements of Upper School departments but rather would be directed toward problems of everyday life. To quote the stated objectives of the course, they were "to guide the student to a recognition of certain major values in more satisfying and healthful living and to provide him with scientific and practical information and experienecs that are helpful in achieving these values." To accomplish these objectives, the student should acquire knowledge and understanding of human behavior with respect to family situations and guidance of children; of techniques of group activity and of their importance in a democratic society;

---

*Op. cit.

of sound principles and practices that affect the health of the individual and the community; of the constructive employment of leisure time in intellectual, social, artistic, and physical activities. A knowledge and understanding of spiritual and moral principles as bases of satisfactory living were to be stressed.

The course further sought to impart certain skills and abilities to the student: to attain satisfactory adjustment within family and other groups, to plan and execute group activities, to cooperate with people of various backgrounds, to manage efficiently personal and family income, to apply basic health principles, and to participate effectively in individual and community use of leisure time.

The appreciations and attitudes to emanate from the course were: an appreciation of individual and group living as a problem of utilization of resources and adjustment to environment; a recognition of the function of the family in developing attitudes that lead to effective living; an appreciation of the interdependence between rural and urban societies; and a willingness to accept responsibility for intelligent participation in family and community life.

The Effective Living program was to bring together materials which would have both immediate and lasting practical application. The first two quarters were to consider immediate and future problems of individual adjustment. Thus adjustment to university life was the first subject treated. The various aspects of personality development and the identification of the student's basic values followed. The first term ended with a study of vocational choices in light of the student's personality and his basic value orientation. The second term was concerned with group living. The family was the principal group studied, with analysis of the life cycle of the individual through various stages of development in family living to courtship and marriage and to the establishment of a new family unit. Since economic problems of family life are an integral part of the topic, consumer education was the concluding unit of the second term. The third term was concerned with the role of the citizen in community life. Democratic and authoritarian means to accomplish change were examined, and the role of the citizen in effecting change through democratic means was stressed.

This, in brief, was the course whch was merged with Social Science in the reorganization of the Basic College in 1952. Consequently the present Social Science course was the result of combining some of the course content of the two general education courses into a new course which would retain the name, Social Science.

Additional sign posts also exist at any university. The objectives of a proposed course in Social Science may be influenced by the administrative organization of the general education program at the institution concerned. For example, the following questions are pertinent. Is the course a required one for all students? Is it an elective course for some students and required of others? At what level is the course to be offered — freshman and sophomore or for upper classmen? Presumably these decisions will already have been made before a departmental faculty starts to work on the subject matter content of the course. At Michigan State the general education program in Social Science is required of all students regardless of their ultimate field of specialization; second, it is offered primarily as a sophomore course though certain curricula require students to take it in the freshman year.

Given these operational factors and institutional characteristics which impinged on the Social Science course at its inception, the course at Michigan State was conceived to perform three primary functions: first, to present a common core of knowledge concerning human behavior to all students regardless of their future major program; second, to provide a foundation upon which the more narrowly defined social science disciplines of the Upper School might profitably build; and finally, to provide a working knowledge of human behavior and contemporary society for those students who complete only two years of college. The program was to be integrated into the entire University curriculum and at the same time oriented toward the needs of the students rather than exclusively toward the requirements of Upper School social science disciplines. In the first instance it was recognized that for many students this would be the only exposure to social science that they would have in their entire University careers. At the same time, it has meant that the Basic College course in Social Science must be broad enough, yet sufficiently specialized in depth, to make it feasible for the traditionally oriented disciplines in the social sciences to assume some prior knowledge on the part of their students. Thus, when the student began a concentrated program, the Upper School departments could adjust both their introductory programs and more advanced courses to the materials he had already had in his freshman and sophomore years in the Basic College. It is with the third primary function as it relates to the other two that a major problem is posed for those who would construct a general education Social Science course. Student needs are frequently so diverse that the needs of one group may contradict those of other groups.

Herein lies the basis for one of the most difficult problems confronting the construction of a general education course. For one group of students, breadth of treatment seems desirable; yet for another group, careful analysis and depth of treatment seems necessary. The one suggests a survey type of course; the other a more specialized course in selected areas. But the degree of success in solving this problem at the outset is crucial, first to meet the needs of those students who will not take additional social science as they pursue their major, and second to satisfy the needs and requirements of Upper School social sciences organized along the more traditionally established disciplinary lines. A related problem arises from within the institution itself. This is the extent to which the general education course is accepted by the faculty of the Upper School social sciences as being something worthy of consideration in constructing their own courses, or the extent to which they feel it may be successfully ignored and proceed with the Upper School courses as though the general education course did not exist.

Objectives growing out of the above administrative guide lines are primarily concerned with the internal organization of the University itself. This obviously varies from one institution to another, and those charged with developing a general education program in Social Science must work within the framework of their own college or university. But guide lines are less clear in a perhaps more significant area. What does the course propose to accomplish for the students who are enrolled in it? Certainly the philosophy of general education gives some immediate guidance in this direction. But within that framework, the faculty developing the program in Social Science significantly affects what the ultimate objectives of the course shall be as far as the students are concerned.

These were the initial problems which had to be resolved before actual construction of the course could take place. The problems having been posed, the next step was to work out an arrangement for attacking them and thus lay the groundwork for the subject matter content of the course itself.

The *modus operandi* used by any department in constructing a Social Science course is in part determined by the nature of the faculty of the department. This is one of the most decisive factors influencing the mechanical structuring of the work load to get the job done. The academic training and intellectual interest of the faculty may be broad and varied or the staff may be drawn largely from one particular social science discipline. Whichever the case, certain considerations are immediately evident. If the faculty is broadly trained and represents competencies in many of the social science disciplines, the task of integrating the several fields into a unified framework may be easier in some ways and in others more difficult. Easier in the sense that several areas of competence are brought to bear on the proposed new course and may thus result in a more balanced treatment of social science subject matter. More difficult because the vested interests of each intellectual discipline need to be satisfied or mollified.

On the other hand, if the faculty represents predominantly one field of social science, less conflict may arise from the need to adjust the course to the demands of those trained in other disciplines, but the end product may show a decided bias in favor of the discipline which is dominant in the faculty. This situation is readily seen at some universities in general education courses labeled "Socal Science" but having a strong sociology flavor or history orientation, thus reflecting the intellectual interests of the staff which produced the course.

The Social Science staff at Michigan State represents competencies in the several social science disciplines: sociology, anthropology, social psychology, economics, history, political science, and geography. Thus the *modus operandi* was more or less determined by the training of the staff. If an integration of the several disciplines was to be one of the prime objectives in constructing the course, then representation from the several subject matter areas was considered essential. But assuming a broad background of training, the second operational decision to be made was the extent to which the entire department would be involved in constructing the course. Two alternatives were possible. A small committee of the staff representing each of the disciplines could be set up to construct the course, or all members could be involved on various sub-committees. The plan put into operation was to establish what was called a Course Building Committee. The Committee was appointed by the Department Chairman and was made up of a representative group of all ranks and subject matter interests. This Committee was charged with preparing a report on the objectives and subject matter content of the proposed Social Science course. It was to submit its conclusions for consideration to the entire departmental faculty.

The work of the Course Building Committee would be subject to such modifications and revisions as the faculty as a whole deemed advisable. The Committee might further establish sub-committees to handle particular aspects of the proposed course — membership on the sub-committees to be drawn from within the Committee itself or from staff members not on the parent committee. This procedure would facilitate communication with the whole staff and would have the added benefit of involving as many persons as possible in the construction of the course.

One additional consideration was involved in naming the personnel of the Course Building Committee. Several members of the Effective Living staff who were now members of the reorganized Social Science Department were to be included in order that the Course Building Committee might have the benefit of their experience in merging the subject matter content of the two original courses.

This was the picture in 1952, but of course eight years of experience with the original Social Science course provided some additional trail markers to the Course Building Committee. What was that earlier Social Science course?

In retrospect, the original Social Science course substantively was characterized by:

1) The prominent part played by historical background,
2) The examination of maladjustments in critical societal areas,

3) The relevance in a practical sense to the everyday life of the student,

4) The emphasis on possible solutions to the problem posed.

While some of these points were to be continued after the reorganization of the Basic College in 1952, yet the new and present Social Science course represents some major shifts of emphasis. At the risk of appearing to be too detailed in examining a course that no longer exists, a description of the course content of the original course is presented here. Only by appreciation of what went before can the significant changes and shifts of emphasis be properly pointed out.

The construction of the original Social Science course necessitated certain preliminary decisions. First of all a value judgment was made. The *raison d'etre* of Social Science within the structure of general education was that "a democratic society can be maintained only insofar as men in considerable numbers can base their judgments concerning public policy, social issues or community decisions on objective scientific evidence." This in itself established the general tenor of the course as society-oriented rather than specifically individual-oriented although implicit is the assumption that individual welfare is best promoted by the same means.

Second, the body of social science data should be integrated into a meaningful whole. The course did not propose to present a series of traditional disciplines arranged in tandem throughout a school year.

Third, the course should not try to survey all aspects of the major social science disciplines. This decision immediately raised the problem of the criteria to be used in selecting the subject matter areas. The conclusion reached was as follows:

> Since the totality of society cannot be examined within the limits of a three term course, only segments of the society with particular reference to American society will be analyzed. Those areas to be selected on the basis of their pervasive nature and their importance to major social issues of the period.

Fourth, although the focus should be American society, some comparisons with other societies at pertinent points should be undertaken. A statement made ·at one of the first planning sessions put it this way:

Our point of view is world wide. While much attention will be given to American aspects of problems, we do not wish to be too American-centered. Universal problems require an international and cosmopolitan attitude for their study.

Fifth, the course should be relevant to the problems of the individual and the whole society.

An exploratory discussion of the original Social Science course resulted in the following tentative draft of objectives and procedures:

This course is planned to familiarize the student with the origin, character and solution of significant problems which confront man in contemporary society. The material for this course will be drawn from the general field of the social sciences with special reference to Economics, Political Science, Sociology, History and Geography. Such information will be used without reference to the particular academic field from which it may be taken and will be presented in relation to the study of these significant problems.

The absence of mention of anthropological data is significant in view of the considerable amount of anthropology which now appears in the present Social Science course.

In the process of disposing of certain major premises about the course, the Committee discussed the question of objectives. Here the philosophy of general education gave the initial guidance to the deliberations. A study of the discussions of the Basic College Committee of the University faculty at the inception of the general education program at Michigan State also helped.

The Committee felt that implicit in the general objectives should be the specific aims of overcoming the practice of generalizing from inadequate data; of substituting scientific analysis for common sense impressions and stereotypes; of critically examining source materials and recognizing one's own biases and prejudices.

But selecting specific subject matter was the central issue. The literature on general education indicates that there is considerable agreement on broad objectives but there is wide variation in specific subject matter content.

The problem of content brought out the necessity of establishing some kind of approach to the study of human behavior.

The primarily historical approach used at many institutions was rejected. But history would not be ignored. "We are concerned here primarily with the present," an early draft of the course stated; "we have a very practical task of understanding the character of this age. Our outlook is distinctly contemporary but we do not forget that the present has roots in the past."

An approach involving a comprehensive analysis of selected institutions in contemporary society was suggested. Some argued that this would be the best way to avoid a survey type of course. But would not analysis of selected institutions be a rather segmented, disjointed treatment which would frustrate the quest for unity? Would not the student as an individual be largely ignored in an institutional analysis? The discussion emphasized repeatedly the functional role of the Social Science course in meeting the needs of the students as individuals and in satisfying the desire for a course upon which Upper School departments might build. A student-oriented course could well meet the first function but might not meet the requirements of the Upper School. This is one of the dilemmas facing all who would build a general education course.

A problems approach was suggested in light of an earlier course in Social Science taught by the History Department at Michigan State. But what kind of problems? Personal problems of students? Problems of society? Or hypothetical intellectual problems?

Personal problems of adjustment were set aside in view of the Effective Living course then being constructed as part of the Basic College curriculum. Hypothetical intellectual problems were also rejected.

The original lists of suggested topics represented a wide variety of subjects at differing levels of abstraction and practical application. They also revealed two definitions of the word "problem." One definition was most closely allied with social mal-adjustment — those areas where cultural change or other factors had caused a mal-functioning of society. This suggests the popular connotation of the phrase, "social problems." The other use related to acquiring information about pertinent areas in the operation of American society — essentially a problem of achievement or knowledge.

The final consensus of the faculty was that social problems in the more or less popular usage of the term would constitute the organization of the course. It would provide a unifying frame of reference.

Once the approach had been agreed upon, it was then decided that the problems should treat some of the most crucial issues affecting the future of American democratic society. Here the criteria originally agreed upon in the preliminary discussions were of great assistance.

One of the original statements about the Social Science course stated the approach as follows:

> This course has been planned to familiarize the student with the origin, complex character and possible solutions of fundamental problems which confront man in the Twentieth Century. These problems are not altogether new or limited to our time. They are persistent, they have intrigued and perplexed man for centuries. They take on new forms and the emphasis shifts, but the heart of the problem is surprisingly constant. These problems are not easily managed, but the present generation must tackle them and arrive at acceptable solutions.

The first meeting given over specifically to selection of problem areas proposed a tentative draft of the new Social Science course. This was to be a starting point. Some attention in detail is given to these initial proposals because the lineal descendants were to be many and varied. Similarity between the first proposals and the end product was more than coincidental. The content of the proposed course would deal with the following major problems:

1. The maintenance of the family in contemporary society
2. The impact of science and technology upon man's work and welfare
3. Community group adjustments in a changing world
4. Establishment of acceptable relations between the individual and government
5. Economic relationships in contemporary society
6. Major group conflicts within society
7. Attainment of security and peace among nations
8. Conservation and utilization of resources
9. The problem of public opinion
10. The development of positive leadership

These items were the begining from which the first general education Social Science course was to evolve.

The Chairman of the Committee felt it necessary to caution his colleagues with the statement that "one difficulty to always keep in mind is that we are not to survey entire fields; that any kind of complete coverage is not a goal. Rather we've had to keep in mind the necessity of detailed study of a few items — items so important that the various aspects may be considered and yet have a continuing study through the weeks."

Having thus before them a rather extensive list of possible problems or problem areas for inclusion in the proposed Social Science course, the course builders then turned to the task of actually constructing the program.

A general student orientation to the field of the social sciences was deemed necessary. Therefore considerable time and effort were devoted to working out this introductory material. What was to be known subsequently as the unit on "fundamentals" was actually an introduction to the study of Social Science as a discipline. Furthermore, the fact that the various social science disciplines have developed a particular vocabulary with specific meanings and usages necessitated an examination of some of the fundamental concepts to be used in the analysis of human behavior.

"Fundamentals" presented the nature of Social Science and the nature of social behavior. Emphasis was placed on an initial understanding of the vocabulary to be used throughout the course and to introduce the three concepts of personality, culture, and society. The intent of these first introductory units was threefold: to acquaint the student with the vocabulary of Social Science, to introduce him to basic concepts in the field, and to disabuse him of certain "common sense" impressions and popular usages, definitions, and assumptions about various aspects of human behavior. This first part of the course was to consume about one half of the first term.

The problems approach then came into focus. Concentrated analysis of two problems took up the remaining half of the term. The first, under the heading, The Relationship between Man and Government, was "The Adjustment between Human Liberty and Governmental Power." Some basic observations about the nature of the institution of government included a historical approach which introduced concepts concerning the origin of government and the idea of the nation and state. An overview of the forms and philosophies of government in contemporary societies preceded an analysis of the character of law and the problem of justice. The emphasis then turned to the function and operation of the American government as applied to the problem.

The final subject of the first term was broadly titled, Character and Purpose of Contemporary Education. Specifically, the question was: how may education promote the welfare, increase the happiness, strengthen the dignity and guarantee the freedom of all men? A definition of terms and a historical overview of educational institutions introduced the topic. But the major emphasis was on education in the contemporary world. A functional approach rather than institutional analysis portrayed the role of education in contemporary society.

The characteristics of the first term of the original Basic Social Science course were, first, the important place that historical background played in the treatment of the subject and, second, the conscious effort made to relate the various analyses to the everyday life of the student. The latter point was clearly not left to the instructor to bring in willy-nilly in the illustrations that he might use in class. A positive relationship was set out in the course outline itself as a subject of importance equal to substantive considerations. A subsequent shift of the entire present course from this original relationship of subject matter to the everyday life of the student to an imputed but not stated relationship represents an important change.

The second term of the course was oriented primarily toward problems confronting society in the economic field. The unit was entitled, Organization for Production, and the question was: how can society be organized to obtain maximum production of goods and services without sacrificing human welfare? An introductory analysis of the relationship between system of production and man's wants provided a bridge to the materials of the first term. It also offered an opportunity to correlate various factors involving the impact of culture on human behavior. The factors of production were then analyzed.

A historical treatment of the relation of methods of production to social organization included a discussion of the medieval manor, the guild system, the domestic system, and the impact of the industrial revolution.

The treatment of production and price system employed the classical economics approach. By contrast, this orientation of economics is significant because the present course uses the Keynesian-National Income approach.

Problems of the business cycle in the operation of the free-enterprise system were explored at some length. The section concluded with a brief comparison of the economic system operative in England and in the Soviet Union.

As compared with later comparative treatments in the revised course after 1952, these earlier discussions were rather brief.

The second major topic considered was called, The Position of Labor. The problem posed was: how may maximum opportunity for workers be obtained consistent with high production, the prerogatives of management, and the rights of the public? A large share of the first half of this discussion on labor was primarily historically oriented.

Agriculture in transition was the third problem area of the term's work. It raised the following question for analysis: in an industrialized social order, how can people who are engaged in agricultural occupations attain social, political, and economic status similar to that of comparable urban groups? Perhaps one half of this topic was historically oriented. The transition of agriculture from a dominant to a secondary position in American society and the impact of the industrial revolution on American agriculture and its attendant problems constituted the major focus.

Three major problems were selected for the third term. In the first, entitled Maintenance of the Family, the specific problem was stated thus: in light of changing social patterns in contemporary society, how can the family more adequately fulfill its basic functions? An introductory treatment of the family as a social institution in a larger social setting preceded a rather extensive historical treatment of the institutional aspects of the family. The impact of social change on the organization and functions of the family was discussed.

The second large problem area was called Limitation of Inter-Group Conflicts. The question raised was: how can inter-group antagonisms and conflicts be reduced or modified in society? Two types of inter-group antagonism formed the principal subject for discussion. The first was rural-urban conflict in American society. A contrast between rural and urban society in such matters as social and cultural life, political life, and economic life was introduced as a preface to the discussion of the major causes of rural-urban antagonisms and of some proposed solutions.

The focus of the remaining treatment rested on inter-racial conflict. The problem of the Negro in American society formed the major share of this analysis although other minority group problems were also identified. The present Social Science course was to delete the inter-group conflict subject as a separate problem area and to treat it as an integral part of an analysis of status systems in a society.

The concluding unit of the original Social Science course shifted attention from modern American society to the world community. The topic was titled maintenance of international peace, and the problem was specifically stated as, Can International Relations Be Organized and Conducted with Regard to the Welfare of all Nations without Resort to War? Again the topic opened with a historical treatment. The economic aspects of international relations included a review of natural resources, the problems of foreign trade, and the rise of economic and political ideologies in world affairs.

The story of the first basic Social Science course would not be complete without some reference to the problem of course materials. Constructing a special course for this particular institution meant that no single text would suffice. The original course was plagued for some time with the problem of inadequate readings. A basic text was finally chosen. But only selective reading assignments were given from it, and extensive supplemental reading materials from other texts, source books, and pamphlets in the Library were used. The students consistently objected to this sort of "shot-gun" approach to reading assignments and this was one of the most critical problems in the early days of the course. It was one of the prime motivating forces bringing about a reorganization of the course in 1951, *before* the reorganization of the Basic College in 1952. The proposed reorganized Social Science course of 1951 never went into effect in view of the merger the following year with the Effective Living Department. However, the work of the Course Building Committee that then functioned, though never adopted in complete form, did constitute a starting point when the merged courses were to be developed as a new Social Science course.

When the reorganization of the Basic College took place in 1952, the two areas of Effective Living and Social Science were merged. The immediate problem posed was to create a new course from the two existing original courses. One was primarily oriented toward the every day practical problems of living, with the individual as the principal focus, and the other was primarily society-oriented with the focus of attention on particular areas where maladjustments existed and threatened the attainment of the goals of American society.

Prior to the reorganization, the original Social Science course had been under study and a process of revision had begun to take place. When the reorganization occurred, the proposed revision of the then existing Social Science course was set aside and a new joint committee made up of staff members from Effective Living and Social Science began deliberations to build the new course.

The first step was to examine the existing outlines of the two courses and find the common denominators that then existed. The areas in which there was considerable substantive overlap, though with different emphases, were as follows: personality development, family, democracy and authoritarianism, inter-group relations, role of religion. Moreover, Social Science and Effective Living were both concerned with helping the student understand human behavior, human relations, and social problems.

Social Science had presented a scientific analysis of the institutional structure of society and the way in which culture patterns change in relation to human wants. In order to do this, Social Science sought to assist the student in understanding the social processes of group inter-action in selected problem areas. Personal values, individual adjustments, or solutions to social problems were considered only incidentally as these matters arose in the process of analysis of group behavior.

Effective Living, on the other hand, had concerned itself primarily with the matter of individual behavior in the social world. Problems which are both individual and social were analyzed with particular reference to the role of the individual and his relationship to possible solutions.   As an integral part of this analysis Effective Living sought to help the student evaluate his behavior in light of the democratic ideals and values of our society.

Both courses recognized that the individual does not exist apart from society and that society must obviously be composed of individuals.   The two departments were thus viewed as complementary in the sense that Social Science was oriented toward certain group aspects of society as a whole while Effective Living dealt mainly with the individual and his relationship to society. It was discovered that in the Effective Living course, when many of the subject matter areas were presented, an analysis of the appropriate institution, or a description of the societal and cultural aspects of the behavior being examined, was presented.   This presentation followed very closely what the original Social Science course was also doing as introductory to the analysis of pertinent social problems.   Moreover, though the focus of the Social Science course was on society at large, the role of the individual was not excluded.   Hence there was a common- denominator upon which to build the proposed new course.

As the discussions continued, it became apparent that a major shift was taking place in the thinking of the members of the two departments.   Perhaps this was the result of the attempt to find common ground from which to develop an over-all framework for the new Social Science course.   Whereas both courses in one sense had been "problems" courses, the new frame of reference was to continue the problems idea but with an entirely new definition on the word "problem."   As used in Effective Living it had meant the everyday practical difficulties of living successfully in Twentieth Century industrialized-urbanized society.   For Social Science, it had meant crucial issues facing the achievement of society's values and goals.   In each, the objectives had been to develop certain understandings, skills, and appreciations of these respective areas. Effective Living consciously sought these objectives to enhance the degree of successful adjustment of the individual to modern society; Social Science indirectly sought the same results from its analysis of the problem areas.   Hence the question of adjusting the objectives of the two courses into objectives of a new course was largely one of shifting emphasis here and there rather than starting out with an entirely new set of goals for the course.

In establishing the general orientation of the new course, the word "problems" was again used but in a way different from that in either of the two original courses. Problems of individual adjustment and problems of social maladjustment gave way to the over-all problems of society — that is, to a consideration of the principal tasks confronting every society. In essence, the use of problem was related to the question of achievement. The assumption was made that "problems" of society stem from the degree of success or failure to which institutionalized relationships achieve the societal needs and goals.

This use of the word problems then posed a further question. Since we cannot, in an introductory three-term course, completely cover everything, what are some of the basic problems of society with which we might deal? Analysis of the following question proved to be a fruitful point of departure: What tasks need to be achieved or what problems need to be solved with a reasonable degree of success in order for society to maintain and perpetuate itself and its culture? Since the answer to such a question is necessarily broad and all-inclusive, some criteria for selection within the framework of the question were needed. The Committee obtained agreement on criteria very similar to those used by the original Social Science course — that these problems, whatever they may be, should be selected on the basis of (1) their persistency through time, their contemporary nature, their commonality to all societies, and their pervasiveness in the socio-cultural scene; (2) the concern felt and the awareness of the problem on the part of society; and, finally, the needs of the students involved.

Once the criteria for selecting problems had been determined, deliberations continued in an attempt to arrive at the central theme. Various areas were considered, emanating from a brief list of some of the principal tasks of society — it allocates resources, it perpetuates the culture, it regulates and controls intra-and inter-relationships, it defines a set of values and systems of beliefs, and in the process of performing these basic tasks it defines group membership and group relationships. Committee minutes observed that "the persistent problems of man and society are grouped around the degree of success or failure associated with these basic tasks of society. The course should therefore proceed to analyze the emergent patterns and forces in man's attempts to achieve the highest degree of success in accomplishing these tasks."

The Chairman of the Course Building Committee observed that "the course should thus analyze the nature of society and the social processes in these persistent problem areas," and second, "assist the student in understanding the social milieu in which human beings live." This is an expression of two different foci. One is more or less an institutional analysis, and the second, orientation toward the role of the individual in society.

Obviously in the discussion of a general orientation of the course, the general objectives of the Social Science course were repeatedly raised. These were ultimately crystallized as follows: to aid the student in acquiring an understanding of the rational approach to the solution of problems which may be achieved through the methods of science, critical, independent thinking, and the unrestricted pursuit of knowledge. The *raison d'etre* of the original Social Science course was also adopted as a worthwhile statement of purpose for the new Social Science course — "that a democratic society can be maintained only insofar as men in considerable number can base their judgments concerning public policy, social issues or community decisions on objective scientific evidence."

The next item was a consideration of the broad areas which should form the substantive core of the course.

A rather free-wheeling, unstructured discussion characterized the first few meetings of the Course Building Committee as it tackled the question of subject matter content. As the beleaguered secretary was to write in the minutes, "Most discussion seemed to center on laying a foundation for communication with each other rather than raising fundamental issues." How true this was can be appreciated only by envisioning a committee composed of an economist, a sociologist, a historian, a psychologist, a political scientist, and an educational administrator placed in the same room together charged with building a course. On the third session, the secretary commented in his minutes, "The meeting forecast the need for painstaking item by item analysis for inclusion or exclusion of topics within broad subject matter areas."

However, progress was being made. "It was assumed by all," said the minutes of the fourth meeting, "that whatever the first topic might be, it should follow an introduction concerning the nature of Social Science, the scientific method and its application."

The minutes of the next meeting hopefully recorded the observation that "despite four hours of discussion which at times appeared to be getting us nowhere, the significant thing seemed to be that the course in its broad topical outline was beginning to take shape." The broad areas were: socialization and personality development, science and the study of human behavior, how man earns a living, and the general problem of political relationships.

Committee members were asked to give some thought to specific topics to be treated "somewhere in the tentatively agreed upon broad areas." Several suggestions were made within the definition of broad areas, some oriented toward the individual and some toward society. Illustrative of the first type were the following: how does the individual become a participating member of society? how do you "survive" in this modern mass complex society? social forces and processes and the individual; the individual and the group; the individual as he functions in society — role-action; the major institutions in which the individual participates; the relationship of the individual, groups, and institutions in the modern world; the development of the individual; the individual and the community. It might be pointed out that most of these suggestions came from former members of the Effective Living Department where the course had been primarily focused on the individual.

Illustrative of the second type, with society as the major focus, were such questions as these: how does society transmit the cultural heritage; how does society organize its resources to satisfy human wants; how do societies regulate and control human behavior; what is the nature of social institutions and the processes involved in meeting society's needs and goals?

It was obvious that many of these suggestions overlapped in varying degrees. The secretary of the committee was asked to examine the various proposals and to point out the common denominators of all the topical suggestions. For lack of a better way, the secretary structured the common areas under four headings. The notation that "the secretary may be guilty of oversimplification," covered a multitude of intellectual sins. The areas common to all proposals submitted were four in number: (1) socialization and personality development, (2) the nature of society and institutional processes, (3) local or immediate forces affecting the individual, (4) the more remote or mass societal forces.

From this variety of ideas, the committee worked out what was called an "integrating theme." It was stated in the preliminary report to the departmental staff as "an examination of individual and group behavior oriented toward the achievement of certain basic goals requisite to the maintenance and perpetuation of group existence." "These goals," the report continued, "provide problem areas in the sense that individuals and groups are continually faced with the question of methods of achieving goals and adjusting to the degree of success or failure which accompanies the various interrelationships so developed."

The three problem areas to be considered in the proposed new Social Science course were stated thus: (1) how to orient new members of the group to the prevailing patterns of behavior; (2) how to satisfy human needs and wants; and (3) how to regulate and control human behavior.

When these proposals were submitted to the departmental faculty, there was general agreement on the approach suggested but with some reservations. First, the principal contribution of the Effective Living course — its orientation to practical everyday problems of adjustment — must not be lost in a course which could threaten to become so abstract that the student would never appreciate his role in the problem area being discussed; second, the statement of the problems seemed to suggest that the new Social Science course was going to provide all of the "answers," in a sort of "do it yourself" package, for society's principal problems. Hence rewording of the statement of the problem areas was imperative.

There had been continuous general agreement, both in the Course Building Committee and in the staff as a whole, that the student should acquire a vocabulary or familiarity with terminology essential to grasping subsequent scientific analysis of the problem areas and that he should obtain a feeling for the scientific method and its application to selected areas of human behavior.

Thus agreement was reached on an introductory treatment of the objectives of the course and on an explanation of the field of Social Science and of the scientific method. The latter was very similar to that which had appeared in the original course, minus the historical perspective. The objectives of the new course were phrased as follows:

> To provide the knowledge and tools whereby the individual may achieve his and society's goals; to contribute to the maintenance of a society in which free, objective inquiry is possible; to contribute to American society's expectations of the outcomes of a college education
>
> (1) an understanding of society and the individual's relation to it
> (2) a genuine concern for the welfare of all men
> (3) a recognition of the dignity of the individual and his right to growth and expression in society.

Then an analytical-descriptive treatment of the foundations of human behavior was to follow. As the scratch pad notes of the committee put it, "we want to look at what we start with." This would incorporate much of the material known as "Fundamentals" of social behavior in the original course — a brief treatment of the biological basis of human behavior, the impact of the natural environment, and a very complete discussion of the culture concept and of the nature of society.

From there the attention of the student would be directed to the processes and systems of interrelationsips through which new members of the group become oriented to the prevailing patterns of behavior. This would be the socialization process and the development of personality. As the minutes of the committee put it bluntly, "Why do you and I behave as we do?" It was in this area that the contributions of the Effective Living course were most pronounced. The focus was directed toward the individual to a far greater extent than in the original Social Science course. The various agencies involved in the socialization process, such as the family, the school, and the church, were to be examined not as institutions *per se* but rather from the standpoint of their function within the total socialization-personality development context. However, the emphasis on the individual was still far short of what some members of the Department would have preferred. They pointed out that unless the instructor made a consistent and conscious effort to relate the analysis of the socialization process to meaningful situations for the student, the impact and usefulness of the course would be considerably weakened.

The subject matter content of the first term's work was thus considerably different from both the original Social Science course and the Effective Living course. "To guide the student to a recognition of certain major values in more satisfying and healthful living" the focus on individual adjustment of the Effective Living course was shifted to an emphasis on gaining understanding from an analytical treatment of socialization and personality development. In short, the objectives of the original Effective Living course were sought as derivatives of analysis rather than consciously stated and overtly presented.

In the second term's work, the decision to treat the satisfaction of human wants from the societal rather than the individual point of view again reflected a change from the two original courses. The problem posed was stated thus: How are human wants satisfied? The major focus of the work of the second term would be the analysis of economic institutions that emerge as society seeks to cope with this problem. To reduce the purely economic emphasis of the term's work and to avoid the impression of following a sociology and social psychology course with an economics course, careful attention was given to dovetailing the work of the first term with that of the second by examining the nature of human wants with particular emphasis on their relationship to the socio-cultural environment. Here the materials dealing with the socialization process offered in the first term provided a foundation for the discussion of the satisfaction of primary economic wants and needs of the society. The consumer education approach of the Effective Living course was dropped. Another significant change from the original treatment of economic behavior in the first Social Science course was a shift from a primarily classical economics approach to the Keynesian-National Income approach. A further change was an expanded treatment of comparative economic systems in the British and Soviet society. Particular points for comparison were selected rather than a complete survey of differing systems.

In defense of its focus on economic institutions, the Committee reported to the staff that "in making this recommended modification, the major share of the work would still involve a somewhat more detailed analysis of the interrelationships involved in the satisfaction of 'economic' needs and wants, but the Committee feels this is justified in view of the major impact of an economic system on human behavior." The Committee further stated in its report to the departmental staff that "The Committee recognizes that the classification of human wants and needs into 'non economic and economic' needs is somewhat artificial in the sense that they are not mutually exclusive." Further recognition of this point would be reflected in the substantive content of the introduction to the term's work by focusing attention on the role of the individual, the role of groups, and the role of institutions in the so-called "non-economic wants" area. The subject matter content would develop such statements as "all economies are based upon one or more ideological foundations; all economies attempt to satisfy the wants and needs of the population as they are defined; all economies organize their scarce resources in a characteristic way; all economies develop some system of exchange." A discussion on the interrelationship between institutionalized ways of producing, consuming, and distributing goods and other aspects of human behavior would conclude the unit.

The essential difference in this proposed treatment from the traditional principles of economics course was its emphasis on behavior patterns as well as the institutionalized processes. For example, the characteristic roles of management, of labor, of economic bureaucracy, the motivations for economic activity, occupational roles, status and class differentials were to be included in the discussion.

The third term proposed to examine this problem: How does society regulate and control behavior? Though the major emphasis would be on political institutions, a political science approach to the material would be modified by bringing in the social control of informal groups, of the family, the school, the church, economic institutions, and mass communication. Social control through American government would constitute the bulk of the course. The concluding material would deal with problems of social control in the world community and would involve an analysis of the conduct of international relations with particular emphasis on the present bi-polar world. This meant an analysis of the system of interrelationships for regulating and controlling human behavior *within* a society and *between* societies.

The basic concepts learned in the first term with respect to culture and society were again applied in a social control context in the introductory sections of the third term's work. For example, the relationship of beliefs, values, and ideologies of the cultural heritage to social control was examined; so, too, the regulation and control of human behavior through informal group relationships and through such selected institutionalized relationships as the family, school, and church.

The analysis of the functioning of the American governmental institution was not the mechanical study of how bills become laws, or the listing of the powers of Congress, but rather an examination of human behavior in the political field. The role of the President, the role of Congressmen, the voting behavior of the people, their beliefs and values as they affect the operation of the government, were all woven into an examination of certain basic constitutional principles which characterize American government.

Comparative analysis of the British system, the Soviet system, and a fascist type of state was to be made on selected points such as the ideology, the division of power, and participation by the people in the governmental processes.

The unit on social control in the world community proposed to discuss the nature of international control and conduct of international relations, not from a mechanistic point of view, but again with emphasis on behavior of nations with respect to their goals, strategies, and tactics in carrying out relationships with other nations. As examples of the basic principles set forth, the foreign policy of the United States and of Soviet Russia was examined. The conclusion of this unit was an examination of the concept of world order. Some historical perspective was retained here somewhat similar to that which appeared in the original course. World empire, balance of power, concert of nations, the League of Nations, and the United Nations were topics included.

The original Effective Living course had placed considerable emphasis on the differences between a democratic and an authoritarian environment in socialization and personality development. The new course, however, examined democracy and authoritarian systems from an ideological point of view.

Course materials have perennially plagued the Social Science course. This was perhaps inevitable; since the course was constructed to fit a particular set of objectives and the subject matter was tailored to a unique problems approach, there existed no satisfactory text book or compilation of materials. The course at its inception limped along with a variety of reading materials drawn from numerous sources. A text book was adopted but it was not adequate. It was not organized in a fashion which lent itself to logical reading assignments. The student was required to read so many small assignments of a page or two from so many different sources that he was constantly complaining of this "shot gun" approach to social science reading materials. It was a valid complaint.

When the reorganization of the Basic College occurred and the present course was constructed, the question of course materials again became a paramount problem. The staff decided to "make do" with available materials for the time being and to give the course time to "jell." However, a long-range project of constructing reading materials tailored to the subject matter and objectives of the course was deemed imperative. If Social Science had been a small operation at Michigan State it might have been desirable to adopt one standard text book and build the course around it. Many smaller colleges and universities with limited staff follow this procedure with apparent success. Yet the breadth of training and the size of the staff of the Social Science Department here made it seem advisable to use staff talent available and to construct reading materials for this particular course with its particular objectives and subject matter.

Two years later, the department brought out three volumes of readings in social science. Unity and continuity were sought through connective or transitional writings between the reading selections. In this sense the books did not conform strictly to the conventional format of a book of readings. Materials were drawn from scholarly analyses, from text books, and from writings descriptive of pertinent points in the course.

The principal problem in constructing the three volumes was reconciling differences of opinion on the appropriateness of particular selections. This involved considerations of both subject-matter and level of difficulty. Once agreement had been reached on these two points, there ensued the usual task of obtaining copyright permissions from publishers. Where permission was not available on an article selected, it was necessary to find an appropriate substitute. In some instances the substitute was not altogether satisfactory to the staff.

These three volumes encompassed all of the reading assignments used in the course. While on occasion an individual instructor might suggest additional reading, the student was required to be familiar with only the material included in the three volumes. An examination of these books will reveal that the quantity of required readings was sufficient for a freshman-sophomore level course without additional library work. In fact, the quantity has proved to be somewhat excessive and at this writing, after being used some three years, the books are in process of revision. Plans for the current revision include reducing the size of the volumes.

Certain selections in the three volumes proved to be unsatisfactory. Decisions made about the appropriateness of some articles have turned out to be honest errors in judgment in the sense that the selection did not accomplish what it was originally thought it would. These will be deleted in revision.

The staff also recognized in using these books that a unifying frame of reference had not been achieved to the extent that was desirable. This will undergo careful study and improvement in the new editions. Recognition of this fact has brought forth suggestions that more articles should be written by local staff; that transitional or connective passages be expanded between articles; and that more extensive editing of articles would contribute noticeably to greater unity of treatment.

In recent years an increasing use of visual materials has also been apparent. Selected films have proved of value as teaching aids in amplifying class discussion and in stimulating interest in course content. Left to the decision of the individual instructor, the use of audio-visual aids has been increasingly evident in the first and third terms of the course. Films are used more sparingly in the second term largely because of the limited availability of suitable films for the subject matter being treated.

In retrospect, the construction of the Social Science course has been made possible only by a willingness of the members of the staff, trained in a variety of disciplines, to always hold the perspectives and objectives of the course before them. This has facilitated the obvious need for compromise.

The original decision, to construct an integrated course rather than present a series of social science disciplines, in tandem, has been a controlling influence. This has not been easily achieved and in all honesty it still leaves much to be desired. Achieving a completely integrated course and one that will appear as a unified whole has been made somewhat more difficult by the quarter system in operation at Michigan State. With the subject matter focused on three major areas, taught in three separate terms, an impression is easily created that three discrete terms of work are being presented. Hence continuing and careful attention to the integrative aspects of the course has been imperative. As the chairman of the department was to admonish his first staff, "Instructors need to be continually aware of the importance of not teaching as they have been in the habit of teaching in traditional department courses. Now emphasis is on interrelations or unity in social science."

Thus, in the perspective of more than a decade, many of the problems confronting the original course planners continue to be items for constant attention. This is not to say that these problems are therefore insoluble but rather to point out that they are continuing on-going problems in any general education social science course. It underscores the dynamic nature of a general education course which cannot afford to become fixed and static. Many successes have been achieved; many are yet to come.

chapter 5

HUMANITIES

*Thomas H. Greer**

The story of the Basic College, since its inception in 1944, has been one of continual change and adjustment. All departments of the College have known this experience, and most of the professors concerned have come to regard it somewhat philosophically. This was not quite the case in winter and spring of 1952, however, when the most sweeping reforms of courses took place. Even those accustomed to unexpected changes were a bit shocked when it was announced, through the department heads, that the seven Basic courses were to be transformed into a four-course requirement for all students. True, there had been rumor, talk, and some study of possible reorganization plans. But this specific proposal had no direct connection with any known faculty study. It was left to the staff, nevertheless, to carry out the curricular decision in a breathtakingly short space of time.

The task of building a new course in the area of humanities, though difficult, proved to be less formidable than in some other subject areas. Prior to the 1952 reorganization, two Basic courses were offered to students, on an optional basis, in the field of the humanities. One was called "History of Civilization"; the other was "Literature and Fine Arts." Both courses were formally abolished in the reorganization, and a new course was authorized which was to "combine the best features" of its two predecessors.

*Department of Humanities, Michigan State University, East Lansing, Michigan.

While such a combination did not appear feasible, the new course did build upon the joint experience of the earlier programs.

The History of Civilization course followed a pattern that had spread across the country in the nineteen twenties and thirties. Starting out at Michigan State (in 1944) as a *world* history survey, it was quickly reduced to a survey of *Western* civilizations. Several standard "civilization" textbooks were tried, in conjunction with a printed outline prepared by the department. The most useful of these texts proved to be Edward M. Burns' *Western Civilizations* (Norton). Instruction consisted of lectures on the topics specified in the outline, plus classroom discussion of the assigned reading. Instructors felt that "coverage" in the course was too thin and the text too limited. Partly as an answer to this weakness, a book of readings was prepared by the department head and a teaching colleague. These selections, drawn from outstanding secondary sources, were first used in 1947 and gave additional depth to the students' reading experiences.

The stated objectives of History of Civilization, initially drawn up in 1944, showed little change during the period in which the course was taught. They called for the development of certain kinds of knowledge and understanding in college students: specific things, such as meanings of important terms in history (democracy, imperialism, freedom), and general things, such as "the historical background of contemporary social, political, and cultural institutions and mores." The course was said to aim, also, for definite skills, attitudes, and appreciations. From his instruction, a student was to "acquire the habit of seeing the interrelationship of place and time," and to "practice drawing sound conclusions from historical materials." It was hoped that the course would aid him in making a "constructive evaluation of the American way of life" and developing sympathetic understanding of ways other than his own. Finally, the student was to gain respect for the achievements of past civilizations and an "appreciation of historical literature."

It is clear that the course and its aims were conceived by men trained in the historical discipline, who were reaching out toward general education with what might be called the "new" history, or "culture-history." The course dealt with successive stages of Western civilization, beginning with Near Eastern backgrounds, then with the Greeks and Romans. It tended increasingly, especially in classroom discussions, to center upon the major ideas of each culture-stage. Although this program had obvious limitations, it was provocative for students, and they generally liked it. In choosing between it and the alternative course in Literature and Fine Arts, most students took History of Civilization. This reflected, no doubt, a certain appeal in the course itself as well as the fear of some students that the "LFA" course was too "arty" for them.

On the other hand, the minority who chose Literature and Fine Arts were usually enthusiastic about what they found there. This course had a decidedly different orientation, was intensive rather than extensive, and was taught by *specialists* in each of the fields of literature, art, and music. While this appeared to some to contradict the principle of integration in general education studies, it gave students the stimulation that an expert in his subject can provide.

Objectives of the LFA course remained fairly constant through successive formulations. The general aim, stated in 1944, reveals the difference in scope as compared with History of Civilization. It was to develop in the student the "ability to enjoy literature and the fine arts intelligently, and the desire to continue, independently, to seek such enjoyment." As a means toward that end, the course aimed to establish fundamental knowledge regarding the "essential content" of selected masterpieces of writing and art and understanding of the relationship of such works to the environment in which they were produced. Out of this, it was hoped, would grow the ability to recognize the "principles of form" common to the arts and appreciation of the "kinds and degrees of pleasure and meaning" found in art at various levels.

As the course developed, there appeared to be a shift in emphasis from the idea of appreciation, in the sense of "enjoyment," to that of "understanding." A statement prepared in 1951 laid down this primary goal: "to sensitize the student to the domain of art by an intensive study of a number of art works." An additional objective was "to reveal the chosen works as the vehicle of insights into the way of life of their respective periods" — and, especially, to "illuminate the contemporary state of western civilization" through a proper projection of works of art. Instruction was centered about the reading and analysis of a small number of masterworks, listening to selected recordings of the chief musical forms, and studying reproductions (colored slides) of chosen paintings and sculpture. Members of the LFA faculty collaborated in producing a book of exceptional quality, to be used by their students in all three parts of the course. This book, *An Introduction to Literature and the Fine Arts* (Michigan State Press), followed a historical plan of organization. Thus, the various art forms of antiquity were brought together in one section — although the student did not encounter them in this way in the classroom. This ambitious effort of the staff aimed to bridge the gap between separate treatment of the arts as taught in the term sequences and their actual historical integrity. Published in 1950, the book had little time to prove its worth before the major reorganization two years later.

When the big change came, in the spring of 1952, it soon developed that the members of the Literature and Fine Arts staff would play virtually no part in building the new program. There were various reasons for this, but the essential one was that the LFA teachers were specialists rather than generalists. Each of them taught only one portion of a three-term course, according to his specialty: literature, art, or music. The new program was committed to the original Basic College principle that each instructor teach *all* parts of an integrated course; this had been followed in History of Civilization. Since the LFA instructors felt prepared to teach only one subject among the arts, it was not expected that they would be disposed to teach the whole of a far broader program. Some were invited, nevertheless, to join in the new effort, but in the end none accepted.

In the circumstances it fell to the History of Civilization department to supply the personnel and develop the content of the "merged" course. Although somewhat dismayed, most of the professors welcomed the prospect. As a matter of fact, the History of Civilization course itself had been moving in the direction of a general "humanities" course. Most of the teachers had been trained in the conventional discipline of history, but their experience in teaching the Basic course led them steadily away from political and economic emphasis to greater consideration of philosophy, religion, literature, and art. This trend reflected the intellectual judgment of the teachers as well as the response of the students.

The problem in building the course was thus reduced essentially
to these terms: how could the existing civilization program be
broadened and deepened to meet the new requirement?

It was quickly seen that a "mechanical" merger of content
with the LFA course was impossible. The two programs offered,
each in its own way, a sound educational approach, but they could
not be satisfactorily combined. The department felt strongly that
it must be left free to create a new course, with its own unity and
rationale. This freedom was granted by the Dean, and the work
was begun.

A suitable name for the new course had to be found. The
name would be more than a designation for the course and the
department; it was bound to affect the choice of subject matter
and the attitudes of both professors and students. Some members
of the department would have preferred continuing the old name
of History of Civilization, but it was felt that this would give
the impression that no significant change in content was really
intended. The name suggested from the Dean's office, History of
Mankind, was considered too broad — and appeared awkward
as a departmental title. The name Humanities grew gradually in
favor. This term was vague and susceptible to various meanings,
but it had several advantages. It most aptly described the areas
of study from which the new course was to be drawn. The vague-
ness of meaning, it was thought, might even invite the active
curiosity of students, who often had a conditioned reflex against
"History." Finally, it seemed to fit logically the general division
of subject matter which the Basic College reorganization had im-
posed. Courses and titles were clearly established for Natural
Science and Social Science. The third piece of the knowledge-pie,
unless major areas were to be ignored, would have to be Humanities or something equivalent. Although the department instructors,
with their history background and associations, were reluctant
to see the word "History" dropped, the majority at last supported
the term Humanities. Definition and interpretation would await
the development of the course.

Committee Organization and Procedure

Once the new Basic College concept was affirmed, most
instructors favored moving to the revised course as quickly as

practicable. The Michigan State faculty approved the Dean's reorganization plan in March, 1952, and the department heads decided to start instruction in the new courses in September, 1952. The first year's operation would be a trial run while students previously enrolled in the "old" courses would finish out their work on the former plan. The change to the revised program would be fully effective in September, 1953.

A special committee arrangement was set up within the History of Civilization department to prepare the new course according to the desired schedule. The key group was the Curriculum Steering Committee, appointed in April, 1952. The department head assumed the chairmanship and reserved the power of final approval of all decisions, but delegated to a vice-chairman the chief working responsibility. The professor appointed to this task was selected for his experience in connection with the outline and course materials in History of Civilization; he also had the confidence of the department. The size of the committee was limited to seven (in addition to the head); this number proved appropriate for its work. The members were chosen by the head in consultation with the vice-chairman. They were proven classroom teachers and were selected, in part, because their training represented various areas of content which were to be brought into the course. One man, for example, was especially strong in philosophy, another in art.

The actual drafting of the new outline was turned over to a small subcommittee of the Steering Committee, but all of its work was subject to discussion and approval by the larger group. The vice-chairman headed this "Outline" Sub-Committee. Serving with him was one other member of the Steering group, plus two instructors who were not members. The procedure was this: the vice-chairman first prepared a general prospectus, based upon specified textual materials. This was approved by the Outline Sub-Committee and submitted to the Steering Committee. Criticisms were raised here concerning one of the proposed books. No more satisfactory alternative could be suggested, however, so the committee instructed the Outline group to prepare a detailed syllabus to fit the prospectus.

Over a period of many weeks the four-man Outline Committee labored. As it completed each of the three terms of the proposed course, it brought that section before the Steering Commitee for full consideration. This was undoubtedly the most difficult stage in the development of the outline. The small sub-committee functioned quite easily, but the range of opinion in the larger group made proceedings slow and, at times, painful. Yet a sound result required the building of the syllabus in *stages* in this manner. The criticisms, compromises, and changes which occurred in the larger group made the result more broadly representative of the training and judgment of the department. The final step, after all three terms had been ratified by the Steering Committee, was to present the proposed syllabus to the department as a whole (some twenty members). At this stage also there was sharp criticism and prolonged debate. In the course of three lengthy sessions, some modifications were agreed upon in light of the departmental consensus. The head supported the principle, however, that the Curriculum Committee should have the last word in this matter. He felt that the carefuly chosen group, which had given concentrated attention to the problem, was a better judge than the department as a whole.

Another small unit, the Visual Aids Committee, worked under the guidance of the Steering Committee. It received from the Outline Sub-Committee a list of works of art and architecture that corresponded to the subjects in the syllabus. The three instructors who served on Visual Aids were chosen for their familiarity with art materials; they undertook a broad search for photographic slides which would satisfy the requirements of the list. The search involved numerous difficulties, but the committee procured slide sets as requested and submitted them to the Outline Sub-Committee. After some changes, these slides were then shown before the Steering Committee for final approval. In similar fashion, the Steering Committee decided upon a minimum set of classroom maps called for by the syllabus.

During the academic year 1952-1953 the Humanities course was taught from mimeographed outlines provided by the department to instructors and students. This proved necessary because of the time factor, but it also had the advantage of permitting additional changes before the syllabus was set in print. Surprisingly enough, very few changes were made as a result of the first year's experience in teaching the course. In the spring of 1953 an Editorial Committee of three was appointed to see the outline through the press.   This group, whose chairman had served on the Outline Sub-Committee, was authorized to make final editorial revisions.   The printed syllabus was ready for all students, as scheduled, during 1953-1954.

Course Rationale and Objectives

The selection and structure of faculty committees played no small part in the successful establishment of the new course.   But the foundations had to be sound philosophically and educationally. The head of the department gave special attention to developing the concept which would govern course construction.

He had the advantage of having served as secretary of the Faculty Committee whose report led to creation of the Basic College in July, 1944.   Thus he was familiar with the range of ideas concerning general education and, more specifically, with the original purposes of the Basic College.   He set out to define the term Humanities as it would apply to the new curriculum of 1952. In a general statement of his view, he referred first to the previous plan of organization, in which two courses had been taught in the field of Humanities.   One of these (Literature and Fine Arts) was devoted to study of form in the arts, with a view to cultivation of understanding and aesthetic appreciation.   The other (History of Civilization) was concerned chiefly with institutional and intellectual history, aiming at better comprehension of contemporary civilization and humane values.   In both courses an effort was made to develop in students a feeling for the Hellenic-Hebraic-Christian-European tradition, of which America is part.

The department head sketched the history of the term humanities.   It had derived from *Litterae Humaniores* (more humane letters), first used during the Renaissance.   At that time it signified a secular attitude after the classical manner in art and literature, as contrasted with the theocentric view of latter-day scholasticism. But in more recent times, the connotation of humanities "broadened and deepened in response to the appearance of a new antithesis." The antithesis is the view of man which has arisen from rationalism and materialism — a view which reduces man to the level of the animal and denies his freedom of will and creativity.   The humanities reject such a narrow conception and embrace those fields of study concerned with men as human beings, as "creative individuals." These fields are not limited to *belles lettres* and the arts but extend to all activities that distinguish man from beast.

Use of the term Humanities to designate integrated courses in the areas of history, literature, and art began in the late nineteen twenties. The programs were extremely varied but could be placed in either of two principal categories. One represented humanities as aesthetics; though presented in different ways, such courses were marked by concern for "art as art, for form as form, for taste as taste." The other category was historical; such courses were organized on the basis of successive cultures. At Michigan State, the Literature and Fine Arts department represented the first type, and the History of Civilization the second.

The head of the department, supported by the unanimous judgment of the instructors, decided that the new course should follow the historical-cultural orientation. The arts and literature were to be viewed primarily as cultural expression, with aesthetic appreciation a desired but secondary outcome of the students' experiences. All creative works, moreover, were to be seen as illustrations of individual genius.

On this basic question, as on most philosophical issues concerning the new course, there was little disagreement among members of the department. This was due in part to the fact that the instructors from Literature and Fine Arts did not join in the "merged" program; the former History of Civilization staff, left to itself, did not have to reconcile its views with those which had prevailed in another department. Happily, ideological questions were rarely raised in relation to course aims and methodology. A broad basis of common experience in teaching seemed to have given the staff a substantial platform of agreement on fundamentals. The historical orientation of the course, the value of teaching from original documents, the intellectual growth that comes from contact with great ideas — these approaches and assumptions were generally accepted. It was understood that each professor would have his own philosophical interpretation of each phase of the course; but all were agreed that whatever this was, the fact that vital ideas were being presented and discussed had cardinal value in itself. This point of view did not reflect complacency; it was a conviction derived from years of individual learning and teaching.

While the staff had a clear view of its aims, it recognized that these were by no means evident to all. With this point in mind, the department head sought a concise definition of the term "humanities" and an accompanying explanation of the nature of the course. He asked all instructors in the department to submit drafts to him, and with the aid of these he presented a statement to the Curriculum Steering Committee. The Committee members found little difference in substance among themselves, but they spent several trying sessions in revising and re-revising sentences and phrases. The modified statement was included as a preface in the syllabus issued to students.

"Humanities is the study of Man as a unique, creative being." Thus, the statement begins with a broad and clear definition. "It comprehends his most distinguished and most enduring achievements — intellectual, spiritual, aesthetic, and ethical — together with his social and political heritage. The sources for this study of man are drawn primarily from the fields of history, philosophy, religion, literature, and the arts."

The purposes of the course were declared to be wide and deep though the department recognized that they could be realized but imperfectly: "to enrich the student's comprehension of his heritage, deepen his intellectual maturity, enhance his sensitivity to humane values, elevate his ethical outlook, and make him intelligently aware of his own worth and dignity, obligations and responsibilities, as a human being." The approach to these objectives was to lead students through an examination and discussion of "those experiences and ideas which from the great age of Greece to the present time have shaped the nature of Western man."

Construction of the Outline

It was the last phrase, quoted above, which gave the key to the course outline itself. No attempt would be made to trace the development of successive *civilizations* as such, but only the development of *Western Man*. To underline the point, a specific course title was set forth: "The Making of Modern Man." This title established the governing criterion for selection of subject-matter. From the principal stages of culture, those ideas and experiences would be drawn which expressed and shaped the beliefs, values, and practices of Western man. Thus, the "routine" institutions, the events which had but slight modifying effects, might be passed over. Time and focus could be reserved for what was the most significant and lasting.

It was obvious, for example, that decisive attention should be given to the leading philosophical ideas of the Greeks, which have served as the springboard for Western intellectual growth. Hence, the democratic community ideals as described in Pericles' Funeral Oration was a "natural" for classroom discussion. The same was true for Plato's idea of the soul, so charmingly revealed in the *Phaedo*, and so suggestive of later Christian thought on the subject. Since our basic art and literary forms had birth in Greece, it seemed clear, too, that students should know the fundamentals of Hellenic sculpture and architecture, the epic poem, and the drama.

From the Roman experience were drawn only the unique and enduring elements of influence. These seemed to be, with little doubt, the conception and administration of a universal state (*Pax Romana*), the development and practice of law, and the building of mighty monuments and utilitarian structures. Since these have served as models up to the present day, they must be understood if Western man is to be understood. Even more important is a comprehension of the Christian faith, the most pervasive single force in the last two thousand years of Western history. Selections from the Old Testament, the Gospels, the Epistles, and writings of the Church Fathers provide a necessary beginning for this study. According to the same general principles, the paramount ideas and institutions of later times were chosen for presentation to students — by means of documents, lecture, discussion, and visual projection.

Simple and comprehensible themes were developed for each term of the course so that the student would not become lost in a welter of events and ideas. The first term was called "Roots of the Western Tradition" and was limited to three main topics: the "Greek Glory," the "Roman Grandeur," and the "Christian Faith." The second term dealt with the "Medieval Unity" and the "Emergence of Modern Man." The third term had a single theme, "Man in the Modern World." In each of these only the contributions of outstanding importance to the Western tradition were treated; traditional attention to political dynasties and national history as such was purposely avoided.

The nature of the outline was influenced in this respect and others by instructional principles which had proved successful in History of Civilization. One of these was the requirement that each professor teach the entire course; this tended to keep specialisms out of the outline. Another was the insistence that all teachers, regardless of their manner of interpretation, follow the prescribed subject content — thus preserving "one course." It was also agreed that the amount of material presented and the reading assigned be kept "reasonable"; this was considered especially important in a program which *every* student had to take. The makers of the outline often reminded themselves that theirs was a "captive" audience. This reflection served to put reins upon excessive proposals.

The lecture-discussion method was continued as the basis for instruction with an average class size of about forty students. The outline aimed to encourage class discussion, chiefly by limiting the number of subjects presented. Countless subjects can be "covered" by straight lecturing, but meaningful discussion takes substantial time in class. The Humanities course had been allotted four class-hours weekly over a period of three quarters; this put a total of 120 class-hours at the disposal of the department.

Limitation proved, indeed, the most vexing problem for the Curriculum Committee. It was always easy to make a case for *including* a particular topic, but most difficult to leave something *out*. Yet the Committee established selectivity as one of the leading principles in construction of the course. This grew out of experience in the History of Civilization. The "survey" type of course had been tried and found wanting. Looking back at their efforts in the nineteen forties, the professors had to smile at themselves. They had started out bravely, teaching the "Origins and Development of Civilization" — from the cave man to modern man, including both Orient and Occident. They successively cut down, seeing its educational futility, to Western civilization alone. But even that proved too large an order. Plans for shifting still further away from the survey were well along when reorganization of the curriculum was proposed by the Dean.

A persuasive influence tending to the "selective" approach had come from the companion course in Literature and Fine Arts. One of the successful features of that program was the technique of concentrating upon a limited number of topics and works. Instructors in History of Civilization were impressed by the method, as observed and reported. When they turned to preparation of the "merged" course, they sought to follow the selective approach as far as possible.

One of the perplexing questions which came up was, "What to do about music?" Most of the Committee members appreciated the importance of music among the arts and as a medium of historical expression. On what grounds could so vital a subject be left out — and if not, how could it be taught? The barriers to teaching music effectively appeared overwhelming. The staff lacked appropriate technical training, and there were few musicians or musicologists anywhere who were qualified to teach the other subjects of Humanities. Physical facilities (records, listening booths, playing equipment) were lacking, and mere "talking" about music was considered a futile gesture.

These were practical obstacles. Partly because of them the Committee accepted with some relief theoretical arguments for not teaching music. The Humanities department was not obliged to teach any *particular* medium or art, and the development of Western man could be explained without discussing musical expression. Since time was limited and music was virtually a "new language" to students, it seemed wiser to concentrate upon equally important, but more teachable forms of communication. It was hoped that some means could be found, in relation to student activities outside of class, to "do something about music." But no adequate way has yet been evolved.

Selections were made by the Committee with easier conscience from the various types of visual art and literature. Architecture, sculpture, and painting were chosen to the virtual exclusion of the minor arts. In creative literature, major attention was given to the epic poem and dramatic tragedy. The Committee did not wish to slight any form, but it believed that a degree of concentration was essential in order to give to the student a feeling for the arts and literature in general.

Related to this principle was the decision of the Committee to teach from a limited number of specific examples, rather than by mere generalization. In the History of Civilization many things had been "talked about," but not seen by the student. The

staff had learned a vital lesson from this dismal procedure. In the
new course Greek literature would be taught mainly by a careful
reading and discussion of one great drama (*Oedipus*). Greek architecture would be confined to one kind of structure, the temple,
and taught through studying one building, the Parthenon. Philosophy would be represented by two masters, Plato and Aristotle, and
the student would judge them for himself by reading from original
writings. Names of works and men were held to a bare minimum
throughout, and students were held responsible on examinations
only for subjects appearing in the outline. Dates and geographical
locations were similarly limited. The aim was to cut down catalogues, rote memorization, and a "smattering of ignorance" —
and to put in their place a limited amount of significant understanding.

The outline, or syllabus, played a crucial role in the course.
In a sense, it *was* the course, for it was made the basis of instruction, assignments, and examinations. Since various procedures and
materials were to be used in teaching, the Committee saw the need
for an instrument to bind them together — one which could be
at all times in the hands of the student. Each assignment was
specified and outlined in the syllabus, forming an integral part of
the course itself. Thus, everything a student read was part of the
instructional outline; there were no unrelated readings which he
might well regard as "loose-ends."

Each section of the outline was a virtual lesson plan for a
particular hour in class. Though instructors were not bound to
this hour by hour, and were free to follow their own emphasis
and interpretation, the plan helped to insure a reasonable pace
through the prescribed subjects. This was desirable, especially for
coordination of lessons with visual aid showings. Certain hours
were designated for slides, and the necessary equipment was set
up in classrooms according to the schedule. The outline gave the
student, as well as his professor, a complete picture of the course.
He knew what to expect and what was expected of him.

Materials of Instruction

The syllabus was constructed, of course, in relation to specified textual materials. A standard textbook had been used in
History of Civilization, and if a suitable text had been available

for Humanities, the Committee would have been inclined to adopt it. However, in that case it would have been only one of the materials used. The consensus of the staff, growing out of History of Civilization experience, was that a text was no substitute for *original materials*. In light of the aims of the course, it was considered indispensable that students see and judge for themselves the creative works of Western man. These works would become the focus of teaching and class discussion.

There was some sentiment in the department favoring preparation of a source book by the staff. Most of the professors agreed, however, that this would be premature. If such readings were to be put together, it was believed wiser to wait until experience was gained in teaching the Humanities. Among source books already in print, the most suitable appeared to be Knoles and Snyder, *Readings in Western Civilization* (Lippincott). It was open to criticism on various counts, but it included most of the works which the staff considered desirable for the course. From these *Readings* the Committee chose the documents which were to form the core of study and discussion. Criteria for selection were roughly as follows: (1) value of the document as a statement of a significant idea or view of life, as an example of literary art, or as original testimony to historical fact, (2) readability for undergraduates, (3) challenge to students and potential for lively and meaningful discussion.

For presentation of works of art, another book was needed. Conventional art histories were examined, but were judged too detailed and technical for the Humanities course. The Committee at last recommended a popular trade book: Gombrich, *The Story of Art* (Phaidon). This work had excellent reproductions as well as simple and clear explication. Its special appeal to the Committee lay in the fact that Gombrich pursued the sound principle of *showing* every work of art which he discussed in his commentary.

In the absence of a satisfactory brief historical text, the Committee searched for some book which might "tie together" the topics of the course. The documents and the art works were fine in themselves, but the student needed a thread of continuity. The search was not entirely successful, but a book was found which supplied a partial answer. Brinton's *Ideas and Men* (Prentice-Hall) put Western ideas in a framework corresponding to the chronological development of the course. Its adoption added a unifying element to the assigned materials, but did not satisfy the need for a more substantial historical narrative. In some portions of the course the outline alone had to provide this, unaided by readings from any of the required books.*

Discussion of documents could take place in the classroom with the source book in the hands of students. It was not feasible, however, to discuss art works in the same manner. The Curriculum Committee deliberated for some weeks on the question of visual aids for instruction in the arts. Charts and poster-type reproductions, held up before the class, had been used in History of Civilization. Most professors at first favored this general method, chiefly because it did not require blackouts and projection equipment. The director of the Audio-Visual Center of Michigan State was helpful, however, in guiding the committee to a better solution. He demonstrated the superiority, from almost every standpoint, of the use of photographic slides. On receiving assurance that the Humanities classrooms could be properly equipped for blackout and projection, the Committee recommended that slides be used as the basis for teaching art and architecture. Four or five slide hours were scheduled for each term's work, and selection of slides was geared to the readings in the art book.

The Course on Trial

The staff commenced to teach the Humanities program with appropriate humility. Each professor knew better than anyone else the gaps in his areas of knowledge. Only by continual self-instruction could he hope to gain the command of subject that would bring solid comfort in the classroom. It was realized that experience in presenting the course would provide a basis for adjustments and improvements. The Curriculum Steering Committee, with some shift in membership, was kept intact to consider and coordinate changes.

The main test was in the classroom, and instructors soon found that the new program was winning favorable response from students. In order to determine this as objectively as possible, the

---

*In 1959, *Ideas and Men* was replaced by Brinton, Christopher, and Wolf, *A History of Civilization* (Prentice-Hall).

vice-chairman of the Steering Committee drew up a questionnaire and proposed that it be issued to all students who were completing the third quarter of the course (Spring term, 1954). Approximately 1500 students were involved, and they were asked to answer freely, without signing their names.

The replies indicated that the new course was generally successful. By a ratio of more than ten to one, students reported favorably upon the adequacy of the syllabus, the amount of subject-material presented in class, and the length of reading assignments. The same proportion expressed approval of the visual aid showings. Most striking was the fact that this "captive" audience, with majors in every field offered by the university, indicated a high degree of *interest* in the Humanities program. Only one student in ten stated that his interest was less than that in his other courses, while three out of ten found the course of equal interest, and five placed it *above* the others. It seemed fair to conclude that the high level of interest sustained, in a required course, reflected a sound program.

Some students (about one-third) reported difficulty in reading assigned materials. The Curriculum Committee had considered vocabulary problems when selecting books, and had rejected a number on grounds of excessive difficulty. Brinton and Gombrich had been subjected to standard analysis tests and had been found to be on the high school senior or college freshman reading level. This was believed to be satisfactory; any lower level would offer insufficient challenge to the majority of students. The documents in Knoles and Snyder were not of a piece, and it was to be expected that a few of these would present serious obstacles to some readers. However, there was no way of solving this problem completely. The department recognized that the greatest single handicap of the students it taught was deficiency in language skills. The results of the questionnaire were a caution against using materials of a higher vocabulary level but they were hardly a warrant for stepping down the scale.

Criticism and Revision of the Outline

The course proved so satisfactory to both students and instructors that practically no change was made during the first four years of Humanities instruction. Revision of the syllabus had been

expected sooner than that, but the need was not considered sufficient until the fall term of 1956. By that time, substantial self-
criticism had come in from the staff, and the department head felt
that a full review of the course was in order. He appointed a
new Curriculum Committee to carry out the task, choosing as chairman the professor who had guided the earlier Curriculum Steering
Committee. The department head, as before, took an active part
in the work of the group and reserved final decisions to himself.

The new Committee was larger than the original one. It
consisted of eleven members, selected for their instructional competence and for their particular interests and points of view. While
the larger size gave broader representation to the department (which
also had increased substantially in size), it made deliberations more
trying. During the limited periods available for meetings, it was
hard for each member to gain opportunity to express his views
adequately and to meet the counter-views of ten others. In the
opinion of most members of the committee, this phase of the work
could have been accomplished more smoothly in a somewhat smaller
group.

When the Committee first met in October, 1956, it reviewed
the criticisms and suggestions that had accumulated. The most
nagging complaint of professors was the one which had persisted
since the Basic College started: still "too much" in the course.
Even though the topics to be covered were fewer than in the
History of Civilization, instructors continued to feel rushed. They
explained, typically, that by the time a document was introduced
and understood, and discussion well started, it was time to move
on to another document. An additional problem was the lack of
assigned reading for certain portions of the course. This forced
the teacher to lecture and thus reduced class discussion. The only
practicable means of meeting this criticism was to adopt some kind
of historical text. This would satisfy those teachers who desired
a return of emphasis upon political and economic institutions, but
the move was opposed by those who wanted to push further from
the "History of Civilization" approach.*

Some teachers felt that the course was an insufficient challenge
to the superior student. For a time the department had offered

---

*The change to a historical text was agreed upon, however, in 1959.

"pro-seminars" to "A" students, but this was not considered a complete answer. Supplementary reading materials were made available to all students in 1956. A special committee of the department ordered books (original sources, interpretative accounts, biographies, and historical fiction) and placed them in a "Humanities Reading Center" in the University Library. A major purpose of this was to give to the better students ready access to an extensive collection of first-class books related to the course. In some measure, the Reading Center answered the problem of the superior student — if the instructor recognized him and gave him direction.

There were some objections to the required texts, but few recommendations for alternatives. The idea of a "home-made" text and source book, prepared in collaboration, was brought up. Most teachers, however, were wary of this: production of a book or books would mean a substantial diversion of energy and a strain upon staff harmony — without assurance that the results would be more satisfactory from individual points of view.

The Curriculum Committee sifted the various criticisms that had come from the staff, and those from students as well. Some could be met within the established framework of the course; others, obviously, could be met only by shifting to a new approach and new materials. The chairman proposed that the committee consider two problems: what could be done to improve the course immediately, and what should be done, as a long-range proposition, to improve the course in the future. The committee agreed to defer consideration of the several long-range possibilities and to undertake a "moderate" revision. This would rest upon use of the same basic texts, with allowance for one or two additional paperbacks.

For the purpose of revising the outline, the group divided itself into three sub-committees, one for each term of the course. The chairman did not work directly with any one of these, but assumed responsibility for coordination. As each sub-committee finished its assignment, the sections were brought before the whole committee. Here proposed changes were gone over, topic by topic and line by line. The next step was to reproduce the revised draft and distribute it to the department. It was then discussed in a special meeting of the staff where questions and criticisms were raised and argued. Final modifications, reflecting the staff discussion, were approved in a conference of the department head, the chairman, and the sub-committee heads. Copy for the press was then prepared, and the revised syllabus was printed and ready for students by September, 1957.

The cardinal issue in the revision was manifest at each stage of discussion of the outline. How far was the course to move from its "history" orientation toward a "literature and arts" program? There was no question of going back to History of Civilization. But could the existing "compromise" position be held?

The outcome represented, on balance, a further shift toward religion, literature, and art, and a reduction of political and social history. This was true chiefly in the third term (the modern period) where the framework of political developments was reduced to the scale already established in the first two terms (ancient and medieval). The staff was generally pleased with this adjustment, but many instructors felt that "historical" content and relationships had been cut to an absolute minimum. This was a sensitive point with most of those who were trained in history and who feared the loss of important values in the course. A few, however, appeared indifferent to "history" as such. They desired that maximum time and emphasis be given to religious and philosophic discussion, literature, and art, with slight attention to social institutions or historical context. This was their conception of "Humanities." The majority of instructors did not share this view. They wished to retain the firm historical orientation upon which the course was founded and had gained success.

Though somewhat divided on the underlying issue, the members of the Curriculum Committee settled upon working principles to guide the hour by hour revision. In order to meet complaints of "too much content," they stipulated that nothing should be added to the course unless something proportionate were omitted. They established as a goal an over-all reduction in topics by ten percent. (This did not mean less required reading, but fewer subjects over which reading was to be distributed.) Reduction proved most difficult because of the usual log-rolling opposition to removing topics from the course. In the end, however, considerable reduction was achieved.

Some new and promising selections from the source book were added, and those which had proved least successful in the classroom were dropped. A slight shift in topics, from one quarter to another, was also arranged.   The outline of the third term was simplified, with a view toward more effective teaching about contemporary Western man.   It may be fairly said, in general, that the proven values of the Humanities course were preserved while improvements in detail were developed.   The advantage of a moderate revision is that it builds upon the lessons of experience with a given set of materials, and permits the growth of educational refinements.   A completely new departure, on the other hand, has hidden weaknesses that are revealed by trial alone.

The department believes in the revised course and expects it to prove even more effective than the previous one.   It does not regard it as final, however, for new books and new ideas are ever appearing.   In time another evaluation will be made, new possibilities explored, and a still better program envisaged.   Courses and professors, like life itself, cannot stand still.

chapter 6

CURRICULUM, TEACHING AND PERSONNEL IN GENERAL EDUCATION

*Edward A. Carlin**

General education is no longer a new idea but whether it is becoming mature or merely older is a matter for concern. At any rate, programs in general education have become respectable. The college or university catalogue that fails to call attention to its general education curriculum is rapidly becoming an oddity. There is a substantial literature in the field. Hundreds, yes thousands of studies have been conducted and the results reported. In fact, there are even schools of thought within the so-called "General Education Movement." Such developments are not surprising nor on the face of it are they matters for anxiety. Most ideas that point the way to change are greeted first as the mark of the heretic and then, if not rejected outright, are submitted to a process of adaptation, interpretation, adjustment, and rationalization until they can be fitted into some larger framework of values, prejudices, and vested interests. Finally, the casuistry becomes complete when men begin to say, "But of course, we always believed that." It seems that general education has about reached the latter point. In fact, we seem to have reached a state where those who are not convinced usually preface their caveats with, "I think general education is fine, but." If, then, general education has achieved wide acceptance even though that acceptance may be no more than nominal in many quarters, and if it now has a history of some consequence, it is likely that some observations can be made concerning

---

*The author is Dean of the Basic College, Michigan State University, East Lansing, Michigan.

its essential characteristics, the way such programs are organized and implemented, and the characteristics of particularly successful programs.

It is commonplace to say that general education programs vary very widely, and of course they do. In certain institutions the program is associated very closely with an increased emphasis on counseling and guidance. In other institutions general education is equated entirely with a prescribed program. In others, the emphasis may be upon the improvement of instruction. In others, the development of broad interdisciplinary courses may be the dominant theme. And in still other cases it has been tied very closely, strangely enough, to utilitarian concepts of consumer buying, food and nutrition, and the like. General education has no doubt received both credit and blame for developments in higher education which need not be and perhaps were not associated with general education at all. Take the matter of improving instruction, for example. Instructors in general education programs have been quite sensitive to this problem. They have frequently irritated their colleagues in special courses and programs by speaking and writing as though improving instruction were either the sole concern or solely the concern of instructors in general education courses. And while general education programs have been studied intensively and while the individuals concerned with them have been amenable to evaluation, here, too, it would be claiming both too much and too little to associate general education with systematic evaluation and testing.

There are at least two characteristics of a general education program that distinguish it from special education, including special education in the liberal arts. First, general education is that minimum of a liberal education in both the arts and the sciences that should be a part of the educational experience of every college or university graduate. The second distinguishing characteristic is that the conventional disciplinary lines are broken, and the focus of such courses has shifted from preparation for additional work in the same area to a course that may be the only formal intellectual experience the student will have in that particular area.

It is these characteristics that differentiate the problems of teaching, curriculum, and personnel in general education from such problems in specialized or professional programs. The inclusion-exclusion process of curriculum development is one example. In the general education program the degree of difficulty in decision-making becomes so great as to be almost a difference in kind in comparison with a more orthodox offering. It is a difficult matter to reach decisions regarding the amount, the kind, and the level of physical science that should be included in the education of a chemical engineer. It is an infinitely more difficult task to reach such decisions for an entire student population. Personnel and teaching problems follow a similar pattern. It is a simpler task to develop and teach a narrower and more specialized course, particularly when the students are emotionally committed either because of special interests or vocational aspirations. An additional hurdle is the fact that in higher education the rewards and the prestige are most frequently conferred upon the specialist who has carved out his own narrow niche for teaching and research. Moreover, the happenstance that general education courses are most frequently found in the first two years of the undergraduate curriculum has resulted in the usual handicaps flowing from the "pecking order" in American education. Further, courses in general education have not been ready-made in the sense that courses in the principles of economics or of mathematics or physics have been ready-made. It is probable that this situation is changing, but if it involves the marriage of general education courses to conventional textbooks, it is probably an unhealthy development. Finally, there are very few graduate programs designed either to train instructors for general education teaching and research or, what is even more important, to encourage a favorable attitude toward such programs.

Yet, in spite of the difficulties that have been enumerated, general education has become an important part of American undergraduate programs. And this is true in the operational sense as distinguished from catalogue and bulletin descriptions. Through the general literature, the special studies that have been published, and through institutional visitation, one becomes aware not only that there are a number of flourishing general education programs but that their common goals are approached in many different ways. When one considers the heterogeneity of American institutions of higher learning and of their student populations, this is not surprising. One institution may have a strong program under the direction of a faculty committee. In another, it may have developed as the result of inter-departmental cooperation. In another, one college or division of the institution may devote all or part of its energies to the program. However, while the details of general education programs may differ widely, including such things as administrative organization, the organization and selection of course materials, and even the philosophic bases for the courses that are included in the program, yet every program that is successful has had certain characteristics in common with others in that category.

One characteristic of a successful program is the courage of the faculty. The development of a general education program constitutes a disruptive force on the campus of any institution. Change may be the only certainty in this life but the deliberate, self-conscious decision to bring it about in the college curriculum takes courage. The college professor with an average of something more than twenty years of association with education is comparable to the man who didn't much like his old hair shirt but had become acclimated to its irritations. Not only does general education as a new program constitute a change but it seems to carry within it the obligation for deliberate, self-conscious, and constant change. Further, the guidelines are not particularly clear for any single institution embarking upon such a course. Programs in general education have had a more than usual tendency to become adjusted to and to reflect the purposes of particular institutions, thereby making their export from one campus to another a most difficult if not impossible task. Samuelson's *Principles of Economics* can be taught at M.I.T. or at a small church-related liberal arts college in the south. This is not true of a general education course in the social sciences.

There is, of course, the grave risk of failure, and on every campus can be found those who delight in making general education failures public. There are genuine questions, too, of the competence of the administration, faculty, and students to carry such a program through. Wouldn't it perhaps be better to continue with the more familiar and orthodox program even if it is not entirely satisfactory rather than to risk chaos in what may appear to be a completely uncharted sea? It takes courage, too, to break the tie with graduate school training, including the special kind of foolhardiness necessary to break through the careful fences that graduate training has built not only around the separate disciplines but around the sub-divisions of those disciplines. There are no instruments that can measure precisely the existence of this kind of courage but it can be distinguished by certain hallmarks, the most important of which perhaps is the kind of disrespect for prevailing custom that is also characteristic of the creative scientist or poet. Mere courage is no more sufficient in the development of successful general education programs however than it is in the successful pursuit of any other goal. It must, therefore, be accompanied by other characteristics, and where the program is vital and distinguished, it is.

One such characteristic is that, without exception, where programs of general education are distinguished, there can be found active, interesting, and well-planned programs of in-service training. The mere courage to change is not enough. There must be direction. The in-service training program can be a first step away from floundering and chaos. It can provide the important subject matter competence and therefore the confidence that the professor may have found so comfortable in the narrower area provided by his graduate training. In-service training programs can and should involve substance, philosophy, disciplinary methodology, and instructional technique. Such programs may be formal or informal in nature; they may involve single departments or divisions of an institution, or the entire institution. They are probably most successful when they reach out to involve the scholarly and research interests of the individuals who participate.

It would be naive to disregard the difficulties that are likely to be encountered in the development of an in-service training program. The faculty may be already overworked with large student loads, committee responsibilities, student advising, and other institutional responsibilities. If a program of in-service training is conceived as being of benefit solely to the institution or as antithetical to the professional and research interests of the professor, it is unlikely that it will engender very much enthusiasm on his part.

This leads to a third characteristic of successful general education programs, one which does not in itself guarantee success but which is indispensable to it — strong administrative support. Regardless of how the general education program may be organized, it must have an important place in administrative decisions if it is to flourish. This carries quite beyond an occasional speech by the president or the academic dean pointing to the significance of and the institution's interest in general education. Administrative support must, of course, include interest and understanding, and it is appropriate that these matters be underlined in speeches or reports to the governing board. It is far more important, however, that administrative support be expressed in concrete terms. Some may deplore the circumstance, but it is nonetheless true, that in higher education as in other institutions there is a direct and high correlation between successful operation and budgetary support. A general education program, therefore, can hardly be successful if it is forced to subsist on the crumbs that may fall from the institution's financial table. Such budgetary support must include adequate and desirable space, reasonable teaching loads, provision for faculty in-service training, for research, for the development of appropriate materials, and obviously recognition in the form of faculty salary and rank.

Each of these characteristics of a successful general education program has a particular bearing upon curriculum, teaching, or personnel. Curriculum development and teaching procedures are matters of vital concern to an in-service training program. Where in-service training is most successful it is comparable to a continuous faculty seminar; it becomes the focal point for much intellectual ferment which may stimulate that probing for causes which is the hall-mark of academic man. An institution or a program that is in this state of intellectual ferment has a great advantage in attracting and holding competent, interested, and interesting persons. During the past five years general education programs have been able to attract and to hold a full share of available educated talent; the teaching has been good and frequently distinguished; and, while the curricula have not been entirely satisfactory, they have held an excitment and a promise that have been most heartening to those associated with such programs.

The future is by no means a bright one, however, because of certain objective conditions on the one hand and because of a probable shift in viewpoint on the other. The objective conditions have all been foreseen for some period of time. They will arise as a result of the huge influx of students that will arrive on the campuses of colleges and universities during the next few years. The problems of finance, space, faculty, and of over-all educational quality that will accompany this influx have been discussed in many places. There is reason to believe, however, that difficult as these problems may be for all of higher education, they may be even more challenging for those engaged in general education. The fact that general education courses are most frequently offered at the freshman and sophomore level means that these courses will be among the first to feel the impact of the vastly increased college enrollments. The fact that general education courses are inter-disciplinary and broad in scope militates against the translation of specialized graduate school courses into undergraduate courses on the part of the neophyte instructor. The fact that the develop-ment of and teaching in general education courses is time-consuming and laborious will motivate many faculty members to seek out the easier paths to recognition that will be available.

All of this means, as has been said many times, that ways will have to be found more effectively to utilize the talents and time of college instructors. This is a difficult task but not an impos-sible one. Visual aids, including television, more independent study for students, additional clerical assistance, and teaching in-terns are all presently the subjects of experimentation, and it is likely that all or some of these techniques can be utilized effectively.

Another problem of quite different dimensions, however, is likely to face general education. This will result from the concrete acts that will in all likelihood accompany the shift in viewpoint that can be distinguished as a concomitant of official and public recognition that the Russians have made substantial scientific and technological advances in the past few years. The shift in empha-sis is already clear-cut. It is, first, a shift toward even greater support of the physical sciences than has been the case heretofore and, second, it is a shift toward more specialization than has been the case heretofore. This shift has been denied, is being denied, and will continue to be denied by the very persons who propose more scholarships for specialists in the physical sciences, who pro-pose additional capital outlays for hardware or a closer linkage and liaison between science and its application for missile warfare. The interesting thing is that most proposals of this kind carry a pre-amble warning that this is neither the time for hysteria nor the time to underemphasize the humanities or the social sciences. Nevertheless, the decisions and the actions that are called for involve a heavier utilization of scarce human and material resources in the specialized physical sciences. In this social climate it seems very likely that general education programs will suffer. If this were merely a matter of a swing of the academic pendulum resulting in a generation of highly trained and uneducated specialists, the situation would be bad but probably endurable. The situation actually is a far more grave one. As a matter of fact, the specialist and particularly the specialist in the physical sciences has not suffered for any lack of support in the American educational system. It seems to be a strange line of reasoning that connects a fiasco at Cape Canaveral with deficiencies in American education. And, even if there is a linkage, is it not with the education of several decades ago? Surely our undergraduates are not to blame when a missile fails to perform. Nevertheless, it is true that if our purpose is to build more and bigger and better inter-continental ballistic missiles and more and more terrifying bombs, we should place all of our national organizations including higher education behind the project.

But is this the case? Has the die been cast? Are the alternatives submission to or domination of the Soviet Union? We and the Soviet Union have harnessed physical science and technology to destructive power more effectively than it has ever been done before. If the curve for destructive potential continues to rise, we must eventually, if we have not already done so, reach the point where each country has the capacity for the complete annihilation of the other. This is not the place to discuss the validity of the doctrine of deterrent power. Nevertheless, as a means for keeping the peace, its logical limitations should be noted. Even if we were to assume that there could be no accommodation and no lasting peace between the Soviet bloc and ourselves, an assumption rejected by this writer, our policies would need a stronger underpinning than that provided by the physical sciences and technology alone. The Russians, as we know, are training not only a spectacular number of engineers and technicians but an even more spectacular number of psychologists.

The point of this digression is to underline the conviction that a proportionately larger quantity of our material and human resources should be diverted into the behavioral sciences and the study of man. But what has all of this to do with general education programs? The answer is that these matters are the direct concern of general education. Mr. Kennan may be correct when he states that diplomacy should be practiced by experts who are professionals. On the other hand, unless there is broad understanding of the methods and goals of the diplomat, his policy is unlikely to be effective or he will find himself thwarted by the misconceptions and ignorance of his constituents. Granting for the sake of argument that the diplomat's estimate of the situation and of the most effective action is accurate, if he dare not take it, the fault lies with the general education of the population. Or take the situation of the scientist. His basic problem has not been one of a lack of public support but a lack of the right kind of public support flowing in large measure from a misconception on the part of that public of what it is the scientist does and what it is he needs. The confusion between science and technology runs deep in American society and is reflected, for example, in the willingness to provide the scientist with hardware and laboratories while at the same time holding him up to ridicule and suspicion for the unorthodox turn of mind that is the very essence of the creative scientist.

The point is that an adequate general education should include an understanding of the nature of science and of the role of the scientist and an appreciation for what he can do and for what should not be expected of him. Many other societal conditions could be cited to support the judgment that general education should be strengthened, but only one more will be discussed here.

General education and specialized education are frequently juxtaposed. And in the development of particular curricula the existence of this conflict is frequently demonstrated. In actuality, however, the two are completely interdependent. An understanding of broad relationships resting upon a strong general education has frequently triggered significant break-throughs in the areas of specialized knowledge. On the other hand, the fantastic accumulation of knowledge and understanding that has flowed from specialized interests and investigations makes all the more imperative the self-conscious development of general education programs if education is to have any meaning beyond narrow vocational training. With every increase in specialized knowledge there is a need for an increase not only in specialized education but in general education as well.   The dilemma then is that, at the very time when the need for strengthening general education has become a particularly significant one, there are pressures developing in our society that may be reflected in higher educational curricula through a diminution of the significance of general education at the undergraduate level.

This is not, however, a time for despair.   There are things that can be done.   Many decisions will rest with college and university administrators.   Developing and teaching general education courses is difficult work.   Therefore there must be compensations in the way of income, status, and facilities.   In-service training is costly but the cost must be underwritten.   The heart of the matter, however, lies beyond anything that an administrator can directly influence.   It lies in curriculum, or the course of study if you will, and the way it is handled by instructors in the day to day classroom situation.   It is in this area that general education programs will stand or fall.   In this area much remains to be accomplished.   This is not to deprecate the very substantial progress that has been made; but, it appears to this writer at least, most of American higher education, including general education, is dangerously culture-bound.   The general surprise and shock with which evidence of Russian advances in science and technology was greeted was a rough index of intellectual isolation and naivete. Our social science is the social science of America and the west. We teach as principles many concepts that have validity only within particular cultures.   We offer whole programs in Western civilization and completely ignore those of the Middle-East and the Orient. Even when other cultures are examined, all too frequently the examination is made in our own terms rather than theirs.   Whether we like it or not, we must know other cultures and our students must be equipped to deal with them.   It is a fact that the great populations of the world lie outside of the Western orbit.   It is also a fact that we cannot ignore them nor can we expect to run roughshod over their social arrangements, their values, and their beliefs.

While programs of general education have met the problems of curriculum, personnel, and instruction in creditable fashion in the past, the problems of the future will require effort, imagination, and determination of an order that heretofore has not been demonstrated. While the need for strong programs in general education is increasing, the forces that may undermine them are gathering strength at an even faster rate accompanied by a surface sense of urgency and utilitarianism. The outcome will depend upon many factors, the most important of which will be the nature of the curriculum that is developed in response to the challenge that is certain to be presented.